Janice

Thanks so much for
your delightful contribution
to Meris "Power of Self"
I look forward to getting together
again soon—

Warmly
Edie Seashore
Dallas 2001

What Did You Say?

The Art of Giving
and Receiving
Feedback

Charles N. Seashore
Edith Whitfield Seashore
Gerald M. Weinberg

Bingham House Books
Columbia, Maryland

We dedicate this book to

Becky
Chris
John
Kim
Nick
Quincy

from whom we've gotten
our most valuable feed-
back

Table of Contents

Part 2. Giving Feedback

Chapter 13: Additional Sources of Difficulty   115

Recording

Resemblance (Transference)

Why Compliments Bother Us

Handling Complimentary Feedback

Implicit Comparisons

Abstracting

Pigeonhole

Assuming

Mindreading

Why Warm Relationships Stay Cold, Once They Turn Cold

Hearsay

Experiences

Part 5. Facilitating Improved Interactions

Part 1

Facts and Fantasies about Feedback

Chapter 1
What is Feedback?

Life is one man gettin'
hugged for sneakin' a kiss
'n another gettin'
slapped.[1]

Most people buy books on subjects they know about, but want to know more about—not on subjects they know nothing about. If that's true of you, then you may already know quite a bit about feedback—that's why you've picked up this book.

It's a good thing when a reader begins a book with a head start on the subject, yet it can also create problems. In this instance, there are so many different meanings and connotations to the word "feedback"—depending on the discipline or specialized field in which it is being used—that each reader may know something different about feedback.

Here is the idea about feedback upon which we are basing this book: *Feedback can be defined as*

- *information about past behavior*
- *delivered in the present*
- *which may influence future behavior.*

1 In the Old West, where inattention to feedback was likely to get you a ticket to Boot Hill, there was a great deal of feedback wisdom in circulation. That's why we've taken all the chapter aphorisms from: Savvy Sayin's: The West is where Nature is Apt to be a Mite Exaggerated., by Ken Alstad, ISBN: 0-99996169-850-0 (1986: Ken Alstad Company 9096 East Bellevue Street, Tucson, AZ 85715)

Examples of Our Definition of Feedback To clarify this definition, here are three examples of *interpersonal* feedback:

Example #1. Alice, an accounting supervisor in a construction company, had an outstanding record for high quality work carried out in a timely manner. She often wondered why other people got promoted to jobs for which she was better qualified. Brenda, who worked for her, also noticed that Alice always came in second. One day, at lunch, she remarked, "You know, Alice, I think a big reason you don't get promoted is that you lack visibility, professionally and in the community." Alice gave a speech on the new tax code at the local chapter of Administrative Management Society, and became chair of the public library board's financial committee. In five months, she was promoted.

Example #2. Arthur, an assistant manager in a branch bank, also had an outstanding record for high quality work carried out in a timely manner. He, too, often wondered why other people got promoted to jobs for which he was better qualified. Brent, his manager, also noticed that Arthur always came in second. One day, on the golf course, he remarked, "You know, Arthur, I think a big reason you don't get promoted is that you lack visibility, professionally and in the community." Arthur was a panel member in a debate on auditing at the local chapter of Auditors' Club, and became fund raising chairman of the zoological society. His opinions on the panel offended a great many people, and his stand on refrigeration for the polar bear cages irritated even more. In five months, he lost his job.

Example #3. Amy, a sales team leader in a recreational equipment company, also had an outstanding record for high quality work carried out in a timely manner. She, too, often wondered why other people got promoted to jobs for which she was better qualified. Her colleague, Bert, also noticed that Amy always came in second. One day, in the elevator, he remarked, "You know, Amy, I think a big reason you don't get promoted is that you lack visibility, professionally and in the community." Amy said, "Thank you for telling me that," but, as she wasn't interested in promotions, she didn't do anything about it. In five months, she was still in the same job, doing high quality work carried out in a timely manner — and quite happy about it. Two years later, she got promoted to sales manager, and was very happy about that, too.

Feedback May Influence Future Behavior Alice, Arthur, and Amy each received feedback about their approach to their work, including things they did and didn't do. Indeed, they each received the same feedback: "A big reason you don't get promoted is that you lack visibility, professionally and in the community." But, since the influence of feedback depends on who receives it, they each experienced a different outcome.

- *Example #1. Alice used the information about her visibility to try some new approaches, and succeeded in reaching her objective, a promotion.*

- *Example #2. Arthur used the information about his visibility to try some new approaches, and succeeded in offending a lot of important people. His reward was getting fired.*

- *Example #3. Amy heard the information, appreciated it for the way it was intended, but regarded it as irrelevant to her career. She did essentially nothing, but life went on, anyway.*

The concept of "feedback" comes from cybernetics, the theory of control. We can see from these three examples, however, that although feedback may influence future behavior, it doesn't necessarily control anything.

What The Process of Feedback Looks Like Feedback in cybernetics emphasizes the concept of a closed loop in a system providing a control function. The thermostat — controlling the temperature in a room — and the automatic pilot — controlling the motions of an airplane — are classic examples of cybernetic feedback systems.

In other words, cybernetics tells us that feedback is a relationship between two systems which can be visualized in a simple diagram:

Applied to our three human examples, what this diagram says is that:

- *A (Alice, Arthur, or Amy) does something.*
- *B (Brenda, Brent, or Bert) notices what A does, or doesn't do.*
- *B responds to what A does, or doesn't do.*
- *A notices that B responds.*
- *A makes a decision: what, if anything, to do about B's response.*

Although the diagram may seem simple, notice that, in the language of cybernetics, it forms a "closed loop." Once A responds to B's response to A's action, then the whole cycle continues around the loop.

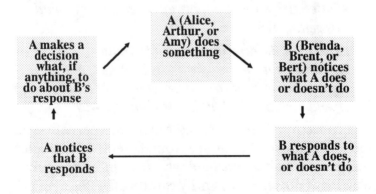

Figure 1-1. The simple feedback diagram

A loop represents a relationship between two systems, in this case, two people. It can go on indefinitely, or it can come to a stop. Once it gets going, the closed loop resembles the chicken-egg problem. It may start with the most trivial action by A, but the final interaction can explode all out of proportion to the beginning.

In such a situation, it's not always reasonable to say that A's opening action is the cause of the interaction. This breakdown of simple cause and effect is one of the reasons that feedback is sometimes so confusing. On the other hand, without the concept of closed feedback loop, we may never be able to understand human interactions at all.

Why is Feedback Important? If we want to build, maintain, or test our relationships, feedback is our only source of information. Without feedback, how could we test the reality of our perceptions, reactions, observations, or intentions? If we want to share our feelings, what other way do we have but feedback? If we want to influence someone to start, stop, or modify their behavior, how else but through feedback? In short, feedback is critical every time we interact with anybody, about anything.

Carl Rogers, the psychologist, observed that one of our most powerful needs is to be heard and understood. Without feedback, what would keep us from inventing our own reality? Without feedback, how could we distinguish between what's going on inside us and what's happening in the rest of the world?

Feedback in the workplace is fundamental for helping those who wish to improve their performance, reach an objective, or avoid unpleasant reactions to their efforts. Feedback enables people to join with other people to achieve more than anyone could achieve alone. Feedback also lets us avoid people who will obstruct our efforts.

Feedback is important for maintaining consistent performance when the environment changes. For instance, now that she has a new job, Alice will need feedback to adjust her outside activities to her new situation.

Under some conditions, feedback may become critical to our very survival. Without response for stimulation, people withdraw, hallucinate, and eventually die. In the work situation, the worst punishment is isolation from all co-workers, with nothing whatsoever to do.

Why is feedback so universally important? Our environment is constantly changing, so we can't survive unless we adapt, grow, and achieve with others. But, unless we can do magic, we need information about how we performed in the past in order to improve our performance in the future.

The Secrets of Interaction Which brings us to the subject of you. If you want to change your behavior in some way, or to preserve your behavior in a changing environment, it's not likely to happen by magic. You will need some kind of feedback.

Why? Feedback is a systems concept. We are used to thinking of airplanes or computers or businesses or governments as systems. You may not think of yourself that way, but you're a system, too. Of course, you're a much more complex system than, say, an airplane. Although airplanes need very expensive feedback control systems, you need the finest feedback that money can buy.

In fact, if you want to make significant changes in your life, you'll probably need something *better* than money can buy. You'll probably need information from other people about what impact you have on them, and that can only be obtained by a process of give and take.

We call that kind of information interpersonal feedback. This book is about how to give interpersonal feedback, how to take it, and how to make the most of what you give and take. It's about sifting the important from the irrelevant, distinguishing information from distortions, and seeing patterns from a series of specific instances. It's about adding new information without becoming confused or incoherent. And, finally, it's about how to maximize the conditions in which you can share your thoughts and feelings with others.

Examples of Interpersonal Feedback at Work Although interpersonal feedback is essential in all aspects of your life, we're going to focus on your work life, where you already have an invaluable collection of experiences. If something you learn influences other aspects of your life, consider it a bonus.

Let's look at one series of examples of feedback that one person might receive at work. Sally is an accountant, and all these things happened to her on one Friday. Are any of them familiar in your typical day at work?

During a morning meeting with clients, Sally corrects an error in one of Jack's figures. The client is angry with Jack. After the meeting, Jack screams at Sally and tells her that she did the same thing two years ago. Then the boss calls her in to his office where he congratulates her on her sharp vision.

At lunch in the cafeteria, Sally coughs without covering her mouth. Willard turns the other way, Sylvia raises her eyebrow, and Jack makes no visible response.

After lunch, Sally interviews a potential new client. The client compliments her on her suit, but later she hears that he has decided to engage a competing firm. Sally is sorry to lose an account, but also pleased because she is sick and tired of getting feedback from clients on her clothes instead of her work. She was not looking forward to giving yet another client a chance to offer more of that feedback.

At coffee break, Sylvia tells Sally that Willard is upset because Sally is too friendly with the boss.

Her daughter's teacher calls to say that her daughter is very upset about the small amount of time she spends with her mother. The teacher wants to know when they can schedule a conference to figure out how Sally can take time from her work to help her daughter make a smoother transition into first grade.

In the elevator at the end of the day, Sally tells a joke. Jack laughs, Sylvia snorts, and Willard pinches Sally's shoulder.

These few examples illustrate the wide range of interactions that come under the title of "interpersonal feedback at work," yet these are only a few of the thousands of instances of feedback that Sally receives in a single day.

All this information may be "better than money can buy," but if you are like Sally, you'll see how easily she could be confused when she tries to use this feedback to improve or maintain her performance at work. Not all the feedback is about her and her impact. Some of it is about what someone else thinks she is doing, or wants her to be doing, or even who Sally reminds them of.

Not only that, but the timing of the feedback is often unfortunate. The feedback often arrives days, months, or years late. It comes in different ways from many people at the same time, or from the same person at different times. And, when it comes, it often finds Sally off balance and vulnerable. Is this familiar, too?

It's not surprising that Sally doesn't always receive the feedback as intended, or act on it even if she does. In most cases, after an hour or so, she won't even remember what she heard.

Or maybe you also find yourself on the sending end of feedback. Perhaps your job requires it, or perhaps you just like to give more than you like to receive. We'll also be talking about why some people's feedback is heard fairly much as they intended, while others can't seem to get their message across no matter how hard they try.

If you're interested in how to use feedback more effectively within an organization, then the place to start is right here — learning how to use feedback more effectively with the individuals who make up that organization.

Experiences

1. Carry this book around with you for a couple of days, and let people see the title. Ask them what they think the book is about, and jot down their reactions, feelings and thoughts — that's another way of getting feedback. You might want to start this experience by writing your own idea of what feedback is, if only to keep your sanity.

2. Recall a situation in which you received feedback that influenced your future behavior. Recall another situation in which you received feedback that did not have any influence on you. What were the differences between the two situations?

3. Recall a situation in which you gave feedback that influenced someone's future behavior. Recall another situation in which you gave feedback that did not have any influence on the other person. What were the differences between the two situations?

4. Before the cyberneticists identified the concept of feedback, people didn't notice the feedback that was all around them — and even inside their bodies. Now that you have been alerted to the concept, see how many examples of feedback you can identify in one day.

5. One of the paradoxes of feedback is this: if the feedback works well, you tend not to notice it. For instance, most people are not aware that the temperature and air quality in their office is controlled by an elaborate feedback system — until the system fails and the temperature and air quality move out of their comfort zone. Next time you go to work, see if you can notice several cases of interpersonal feedback that are only noticed because they stopped functioning well.

Chapter 2
Models of Feedback

> *When wiser men are
> talkin', let your ears hang
> down and listen.*

Over our years of consulting and training people to improve their interaction skills, we have used several helpful models. In order to improve your skills, or help others, you may want to master these models, too. If you don't understand why you might need a model to help you improve interaction skills, recall the last time you were mystified by what ought to have been a simple interaction. You asked for the time of day and got criticized for the tie you were wearing. Someone innocently handed you the day's mail and you snapped at him. You and your roommate were discussing where to go to lunch and suddenly you were arguing about who emptied the wastebasket three months ago.

When such interactions take place, they generally happen so fast we just remain mystified. To slow down this lightning-fast process and make it easier to see what's going on inside, we can use a step-by-step model of interaction.

In our work with interpersonal feedback, we have used the contributions of many people, but particularly several theorists whose works have helped us understand the secrets of interaction. The following are some of our thoughts about the contributions of Sigmund Freud, Joe Luft and Harry Ingham, Norbert Weiner, Kurt Lewin, Carl Rogers, and Virginia Satir, We have integrated their work into our theories of interpersonal feedback, and in so doing, we have transformed or twisted them to suit our own purposes, perhaps beyond easy recognition. In any case, our interpretations are not their responsibility, but only ours.

Many of our readers will be well acquainted with these models, so at this early stage we will give the briefest of summaries as a reminder. For those readers who are less familiar, we have placed longer summaries in appendices, or references to the original works and some extensive interpretations.

Sigmund Freud

The work of Sigmund Freud underlies just about everything since written about human interaction, and we could not begin to elaborate all the ways. Let's give just a few important examples.

The Freudian concept of "defense mechanisms" talks about the way that you defend yourself against my messages as if your very survival is at stake.

The Freudian term "projection" refers to the way I place an image of what's inside of me onto you, as if you were a screen and I were a film projector. Projection leads me to send you a message which tells mostly about me, and could or could not have anything to do with you.

Perhaps Freud's most important influence on interpersonal feedback thinking is the concept of the "unconscious." The "Freudian slip" is one way that Freud illustrated that there were parts of our minds that contain things that we don't know are there. I might say "I'd like to kiss — I mean kick — you for that." The "kiss" that slips out may tell you more about me than I wanted you to know, or even knew myself.

Joe Luft and Harry Ingham

Many thinkers have taken up Freud's insights into the known and unknown areas of the mind. Joe Luft and Harry Ingham's "Johari Window," shown in Figure 2.1, delineates four categories of information involved in interpersonal feedback. The *open area* is what we both share about what we know about me. The *hidden area* is what I hide from you about what is going on inside of me.

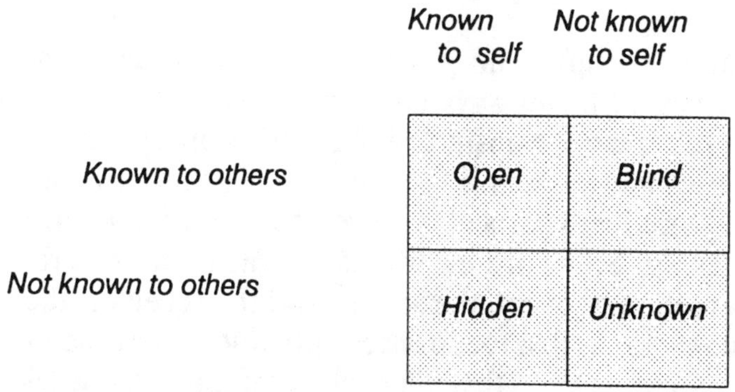

	Known to self	Not known to self
Known to others	Open	Blind
Not known to others	Hidden	Unknown

Figure 2.1 The Johari Window

In the *blind area,* you keep from me what you observe about me, or think or feel about me, that I don't know about. In the *unknown area,* there is a part of me, from my past, which neither one of us yet knows about, at least on a conscious level. Part of this is Freud's unconscious, from which information might suddenly "pop out" in our interaction, surprising us both.

Norbert Weiner

Norbert Weiner was a mathematical prodigy who was to cybernetics what Freud was to psychoanaiysis. During World War II, Weiner's work on feedback mechanisms helped the military to improve the accuracy of fire on moving targets. After the war, Weiner became preoccupied with the use of his ideas for peace and human betterment. He generalized the concepts of cybernetics — Greek for "the science of steersmanship" — to everything from thermostats to governing the world. His ideas generated a wildfire of intellectual activity, and were influential in altering the face of many science and engineering fields.

Kurt Lewin

One of the people who picked up Weiner's ideas was Kurt Lewin, in many ways the "father of interpersonal feedback." Lewin transferred Weiner's concepts from cybernetics into human interaction, thus giving it a significant place in all parts of our lives, from our workplace to our family. Some of Lewin's main contributions were: the interaction between the sender and the receiver; the kinds of resources that feedback can provide for our maintenance, survival, growth and development; and the ways we can continue to be more skillful in the use of this enormously critical concept and tool. Lewin is especially noted as the founder of "action research" — the use of real human learning groups as laboratories in which to study interaction.

Carl Rogers

Carl Rogers has influenced all modern theorists of human interaction, first with his concept of unconditional positive regard for every person. Especially important is his idea of my reflecting back to you your thoughts and feelings as feedback to you, leaving out any of my own interpretations and judgments. This kind of reflective listening provides a kind of neutral baseline against which all other forms of feedback can be measured. Figure 2.2 shows an interaction between a person and a computer program, Eliza, by Jerome Weizenbaum, which approximates the reflective listening of a Rogerian therapist.

> **Eliza:** *How do you do. Please tell me your problem.*
> **Patient:** Everybody says I'm a wimp.
> *Really, everybody?*
> Well, almost everybody.
> *Surely not everybody.*
> You're right.
> *What makes you think I am right?*
> You are much smarter than I am.
> *Does it please you to believe I am much smarter than you are?*
> It would please me if you were my friend.
> *Do you think it likely that I was your friend?*
> Yes.
> *You seem to be quite positive.*
> I'm not sure.
> *Is it because you are not sure that you came to me?*
> Yes, I am a wimp.
> *You are sure.*
> No, but my mother told me I am a wimp.
> *Are you saying no just to be negative?*
> I'm repeating what my mother told me.
> *Tell me more about your family.*
> My father was a wimp, too.
> *Who else in your family was a wimp?*
> Just me.
> *Let's discuss further why your mother told you.*
> My mother loves me.
> *Your mother?*
> ...

Figure 2.2 Rogerian reflective listening simulated by acocomputer program, Eliza, interacting with a human being.

Notice how the computer, in the guise of therapist, really adds nothing substantive to the interaction, so that whatever comes out — love, sex, family relationships, feelings of confidence or lack of confidence — all must be coming from the patient, not the "therapist." Surprisingly, this interaction sometimes shows remarkable "insight" and startling "interventions," like when the therapist puts the patient in a "double bind" by asking him if he's sure he's a wimp. If he's sure he's a wimp, then he's not being wimpy, but if he's not sure, then he is.

Virginia Satir

Virginia Satir has been called "the Columbus of family therapy." She took ideas from Freud, Rogers, Weiner, Lewin, and, as she said, "any place I could find help," and synthesized them into many models to use in helping dysfunctional families cope more congruently with their problems. Her Interaction Model (see Figure 2.3) can be summarized from two perspectives. I send you a message, which you perceive and interpret in any way you choose. You then have your own feeling about your interpretation, and immediately thereafter, you have a feeling about that feeling. After first filtering all of this internal material through your rules about commenting, you may share none, any, or all of it with me.

I have no idea what happened to my message until you let me know, or I see behavior from you, which I then choose to perceive and interpret in my own fashion, and then continue to go though the same cycle inside of me: a message sent, perception and interpretation made, a feeling produced, and immediately after, a feeling about that feeling, eventually leading to my sharing with you.

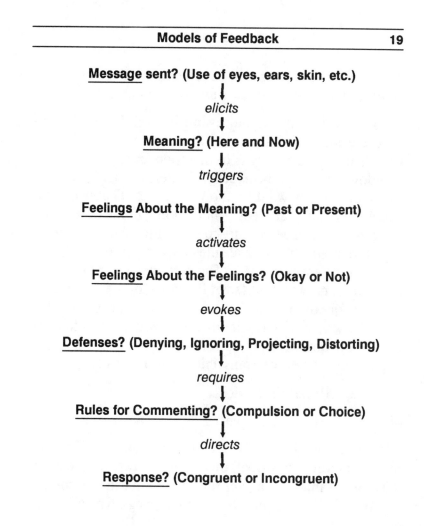

Message sent? (Use of eyes, ears, skin, etc.)

↓

elicits

↓

Meaning? (Here and Now)

↓

triggers

↓

Feelings About the Meaning? (Past or Present)

↓

activates

↓

Feelings About the Feelings? (Okay or Not)

↓

evokes

↓

Defenses? (Denying, Ignoring, Projecting, Distorting)

↓

requires

↓

Rules for Commenting? (Compulsion or Choice)

↓

directs

↓

Response? (Congruent or Incongruent)

Figure 2.3 Satir's Interaction Model reveals the   ii **internal part of the feedback process from receipt of message to sending the next message**

It's Not As Bad As It Seems

If it really takes so many models to understand feedback, perhaps it's not worth the trouble. Will you need a book or a reference library every time you ask for the time of day? Not really. It's just that the models we use must be powerful enough to enable us to decipher the worst case, whereas most interactions aren't that complicated.

Most interactions are quite simple, even in the view of all these models. You start by asking, sincerely, "What time is it?" Everything is in the open area of the Johari Window, I hear it all correctly. I interpret what you said to mean that you want to know the time. That was what you meant, and it arouses a mild feeling in me of wanting to help you. I have no particular feeling about this feeling, so none of my survival rules have been touched, and no defenses are necessary. The response I want to make is to look at my watch and say, "It's three forty-five." I have no rules for commenting that prevent me from saying this just that way, and I have no unrecognized feelings to contribute uncontrollable non-verbal response to the message. Thus, the entire transaction goes like this:

You say, "What time is it?"

I say, "It's three forty-five."

We don't need Freud's defenses, the Johari Window, Satir's Interaction Model, or any of the rest to decipher this kind of interaction, yet this is the kind that accounts for about 99% of all our interactions during a typical working day.

...It's Worse

Unfortunately, the simple, straight interactions do not account for 99% of our *time* during the working day, because they just happen in a few seconds and then are forgotten. The most complex kind of interactions may account for less than 1% of our interactions during a typical working day. Yet, because we cannot untangle them, or untangle ourselves from them, we find ourselves spending half our time, or more, in such unproductive interactions.

That's why a model is so valuable. We don't need it every minute, but when we do need it, it may save us hours or even days of wrestling with a tangled situation. One of the reasons we can be effective as consultants is that we know how to apply models to situations where our clients have gotten stuck.

In between the two extremes there are interactions that are not crystal-clear, but aren't totally tangled, either. These interactions also take a disproportionate amount of our working time, though they may not be as frustrating as the worst ones. This is also the type of interaction that responds best to analysis based on the models. Usually, all we need to do is identify the single step in which the processing started to deviate from the clear path. Once we get that one step in order, we can get the interaction back on track.

Experiences

1. What other models do you regularly use to help you in understanding human interaction? What writers have particularly influenced you in the way you deal with other people?

2. Choose one of the models we have suggested and apply it to an interaction situation you are currently confused by, in your personal life or at work.

Part 2

Giving Feedback

Many of our fantasies about feedback interactions come from our childhood. When feedback was given to us by those more powerful, we were supposed to take it, believe it, and change our behavior in accordance with it. The giver was out to help us; it was feedback "for our own good."[1]

All children are born small. Though some of us may grow up to be big and powerful, we all share the experience of being little and weak — and surrounded by powerful giants. When the giants spoke, we listened. The principal fantasy about giving feedback derives from these childhood experiences.

---

[1]Alice Miller, <u>For Your Own Good: Hidden cruelty in child-rearing and the roots of violence,</u> (New York: Farrar, Straus, Giroux, 1983) shows dramatically what happens when this kind of feedback is also uniformly critical.

The Giver's Fantasy: *If feedback has all the correct ingredients in its delivery — clear, specific, timed right, nonjudgmental, and speaks only to behavior — it will be accepted as given.*

Only later in life did we learn that this is a fantasy, and many of us did not learn — at least we didn't learn for all occasions. But once we understand Satir's Interaction Model, we understand that The Giver's Fantasy must be a fantasy, because the response of the receiver has an almost completely arbitrary connection with what the giver sent.

On the other hand, because we were children, we had little experience with growth processes. We believed that our house had always been there, because it was there all our lives, and we believed that our parents had always been perfectly formed grownups. Being perfectly formed grownups, everything they said had to be what it seemed to be, so when they told us something like, "You're not trying hard enough," or "You're making me angry," we believed that these were statements about us. As the interaction model shows, however, the facts were quite different, and most of what they were telling us was not about us, but about them.

The Giver's Fact: *No matter what it appears to be, feedback information is almost totally about the giver, not the receiver.*

In this part, we'll examine these and other facts and fantasies about giving feedback.

Chapter 3
The Compulsion to Give Feedback

*The best way to convince
a tenderfoot is to let him
have his own way.*

Even When Requested, Feedback Describes the Giver.
Jerry was giving a workshop in Lincoln, where he lives. It
was the first time he had given this particular workshop,
and he was quite anxious about how well it had gone.

At the end of the first day, Jerry gave Foster a ride home.
While they rode, he asked Foster, "How did it go?"

Foster said, "Jerry, there's only one thing that I don't
understand out of our discussion today."

"And what's that?" Jerry asked.

"If you're such a good consultant, why do you drive such
an old car?"

Jerry may have thought he was asking for feedback about
his workshop, or about himself. Instead, he got information about Foster. This suggests the first of **The Giver's
Facts:**

*Even when it's given at the receiver's request, feedback
describes the giver more than the receiver.*

Why should this be so? Satir's Interaction Model gives us some clues.

1. The giver only perceives certain aspects of the receiver's behavior. No one can give feedback on behaviors that are outside his perception.

2. Second, the giver then organizes these perceptions in ways that are meaningful to her. No one will comment on things that she does not see as having meaning.

3. The giver selects certain aspects out of thousands that might be commented upon, according to the emotional reaction triggered in him. Foster happened to be interested in new cars that day.

4. The giver's inner feelings and rules for commenting determine the style, choice of words, emotional tone, and non-verbal cues that comprise the entire feedback package.

All of this provides information on how the giver sees and behaves toward other people. In fact, clever individuals often seek feedback solely to diagnose the giver, paying little or no attention to the content as it applies to them.

The Giver's Fact says we reveal ourselves by giving feedback. Don't we respect our privacy enough that we wouldn't be willing to reveal so much? So why don't we keep our feedback to ourselves? The simple truth is that we cannot help ourselves.

The Second Most Essential Human Need. Giving feedback seems to be the second most essential ingredient of life itself — after air, and before water. Humans can live for about three minutes without air, three days without water, and three months without food. But according to our observations, most people cannot live more than three hours without offering someone else an observation about themselves — often in the form of advice.

Although we cannot hope to eliminate so fundamental a need, we might be able to help you tame your impulses. If we could stretch the three hours to four, or slow the reflex long enough for you to shape the feedback more appropriately, then we will have made an immense contribution to human welfare. Perhaps the following facts about helping others will help you not be so impatient to be helpful.

Nobility Isn't Good Enough We often think since we're trying to *help* by giving feedback, it will be easy to succeed. As a result, we often get careless.

Fact: *Wanting to help people may be a more noble motive than some, but that doesn't make feedback any easier.*

Any time someone asks you for feedback — or even worse, pays you — you tend to think how smart and good you are, and you get careless. Giving or receiving feedback effectively is always hard work. Carelessness in feedback is a sure ticket to disaster.

They Have to Want It If you're not absolutely sure they want your feedback, it's best to check it out. One way to check it out is by asking, which we seldom ever bother to do.

Fact: *If people don't want your feedback, you'll never succeed in reaching them, no matter how smart or wonderful you are.*

We stress the importance of not giving uninvited feedback, not because it's morally wrong, but because *it doesn't work.* It's okay to do it if you don't care about your relationship with the other person or about wasting your own time. Indeed, that's a pretty good description of the type of situation in which we slip into giving unsolicited feedback: *We don't really care about the other person, and we don't have anything very useful to do with our time.*

No Invitation is Forever Even when you care about people, and they ask you for feedback, when they discover what your feedback will cost them, they may change their minds. Once we start to give feedback, we often fail to recognize obvious clues that our feedback is no longer welcome.

What are such obvious clues? As the interaction advances, you may find yourself growing progressively more rude, impatient, and suspicious. If you feel that way toward someone you're trying to help, perhaps you're sensing that they don't want you any longer.

Fact: *Even when people agree that they want your help, that agreement is not usually a lifetime contract.*

When you agree to provide feedback, you're not committed to continue giving it. You are committed to continue monitoring the situation to discover when the feedback is no longer wanted. And then to stop.

Some Things Are Worse Than Failure Just stopping seems hard to do, especially when "just one last word" will patch up the worsening situation. Whenever you find yourself thinking things couldn't get a lot worse, just remember that they can—a lot worse.

Fact: *Even when you agree to give feedback to someone, that agreement need not be a lifetime contract. You're allowed to stop when you've had enough.*

It's all right to admit you failed in your generosity, especially if it helps you stop before you make things a lot worse.

You Ain't No Saint People who want to give feedback to other people generally expect to get something out of it for themselves—though they may not be aware of it. Before you yield to the temptation to give feedback, become aware of it.

Fact: *There are very few living saints—at least, we've never had the pleasure of meeting any.*

Most people agree that this fact applies to other people. Few people realize it applies to them. Certainly not any of your authors.

The Best Use of Giving Feedback Giving feedback is often a way of exercising influence via the Trojan Horse. It looks as though it is for the benefit of the receiver but disguises the payoff to the sender. Regardless of the utility to the receiver, such feedback serves as a convenient vehicle for avoiding, displacing, attacking, gaining status, and justifying the status quo for the sender.

Fortunately for world peace, receivers can usually sense the existence of hidden motives in feedback. When they do, there's little chance of their accepting the ostensible message, so if you're *really* interested in helping people, you'll do well to start your feedback by opening your own motives to inspection, perhaps by using the interaction model.

Of course, this seems a rather tedious way to start feedback, but most of the time, introspection and care with words will be far more efficient and effective than sending Trojan Horse Feedback. More often than not, however, we stop short of a full explanation and settle for something quick, easy, comfortable, compatible, or self-limiting.

As a sender, your best use of feedback is to note your impulse to give, then reflect on what is going on inside you.

What is it that makes offering feedback such an appealing alternative among the unlimited opportunities of other things you might do to improve your relationships? Have you become a feedback junkie, and forgotten that there are other ways?

Experiences

1. What is it for *you* that makes offering feedback such an appealing alternative?

2. Charlie's favorite example of the fate of uninvited feedback is the way Edie extols the merits of closing the cupboard door after he gets his orange juice glass out in the morning. Even though it is not a big deal, and even though he thinks she has a good idea, he is amazed at the frequency with which the issue recurs. Actually, Charlie is embarrassed. He also thinks Edie is disgusted. What is worse, he thought the cupboard door was the important issue — only to find out recently that not putting the orange juice back in the refrigerator is what's really bugging her.

Individual items of feedback may not be terribly important, but if there is a pattern of repeated feedback, there may be some important message hidden in it, a message that is not being effective. You can probably recall a piece of feedback that, like Charlie's, you've heard over and over and over and over and over again. Review the situation and see if you can explain why it never has the desired effect — and perhaps why it has the opposite effect.

3. Can you recall a piece of feedback that you've given over and over and over and over and over again? Review the situation and see if you can explain why it never has the desired effect — and perhaps why it has the opposite effect. What might you do differently?

Chapter 4
Giving Feedback When Invited

| *Silence can be a speech.*

The first and most essential question when we're teetering on the brink of giving feedback is:

Have they asked me to give them personal information?

If the answer is "no," then if you feel compelled to give it anyway, you'd be wise to question your motives — and so would the receiver. In this chapter, we'll take up the situation when the answer to this question is "yes," meaning there's actually been some kind of invitation to give feedback.

Directly Paid Invitations. The easiest way to recognize an invitation to give feedback is when someone pays you to do it, but even then it's difficult. In many organizations, management pay consultants thousands of dollars to "tell us the truth," then engage in a life-and-death struggle to prevent any information about management from getting through.

People resist feedback in exactly the same way when they hire a therapist — doctor, psychologist, psychiatrist, marriage counselor, or whatever they call them. And, when they come to an experiential workshop with the same objective, they invariably put up the same kind of strong resistance.

Fact: *Just because you're a paid consultant, therapist, or workshop facilitator, you still can't take the invitation to give feedback for granted.*

As you're about to say something, remember that when they paid you, they probably weren't thinking of *that* feedback.

Indirectly Paid Invitations. Sometimes we are paid to give feedback, but not by the person who is to receive it. Judges and police give this kind of third-party feedback, which may be why it tends to be so poorly received.

Schoolteachers and court-appointed therapists also find themselves in this kind of third-party relationship. So do consultants who are paid by managers to tell employees just what they are doing wrong.

Managers themselves are in the same relationship to their employees. They are paid by the owners of the business to see that the employees work effectively. By accepting a paycheck, an employee implicitly accepts a certain amount of third-party feedback. Employees, however, don't always perceive the transaction that way, and often consider management feedback to be unsolicited.

Handling Indirectly Paid Invitations. The person who is paid by a third party to give feedback is in a tough position, tougher in fact than the person who simply gives unsolicited feedback. The person who is paid directly is not that much better off. If you find yourself in either of these positions, there's one cardinal rule.

Fact: *Feedback that's not absolutely relevant to the task you're paid for will not be accepted, and even worse, will interfere with that task.*

If you're a judge, keep silent on the felon's religious beliefs.

If you're a doctor, don't give your patients advice on how to dress.

If you're a schoolteacher, hold your tongue about the students' friends outside school.

If you're a manager, refrain from commenting on how your employees spend their evenings.

In each of these situations, you could probably make a case for the potential relevance of the feedback. As a judge, you probably believe that a felon would be more law-abiding if he became a devout Christian, but your job as judge is law, not Christianity. As a doctor, you might feel that your patient would get a better job if he dressed more appropriately, but your job is health, not job counseling. As a teacher, you might feel your student would get better grades if she hung around with a more serious crowd, but your job is teaching, not social directing.

As a manager, you might notice an employee yawning and not paying attention in an important meeting. You might be tempted to comment on how she spends her evenings, but it's a terrible idea. If you feel a comment is called for, comment on her not paying attention in the meeting, which is part of her job — and yours. Her evenings are none of your business; her job performance is.

There are many excellent business reasons for not offering this kind of comment on her personal life. If you comment on her evenings, she may get angry, tell you to mind your own business, and entirely miss your point about job performance. She may misinterpret your intentions, and think you want to get involved in her personal life. It's especially important to be clear about your intentions, for there have been numerous cases where managers were more interested in a staff member's personal life than in her job performance.

But even if she keeps all that clear, and takes your comment to heart, you've now created a potential confusion of roles. As a result, the next time you offer some feedback that's directly relevant to your role as her manager, she may regard it as personal, and decide to ignore it.

Yes, in each of these situations, you could probably make a case for the potential relevance of the feedback.

Fact: *If you have to make a case for the task-relevance of your feedback, you probably don't have a case, and you certainly won't have any success.*

Friendly Invitations. Once we've dealt the paid feedback, we're left with the freebies. These are the cases where friends or colleagues simply ask for feedback as a favor, or respond affirmatively to a friendly offer of feedback. Such unpaid invitations make up by far the largest numbers of feedback situations, and each example is different:

1. *I'd like your honest opinion of my new manuscript.*

2. *Does this tie go with this shirt?*

3. *Do you think I made a good impression on the boss?*

About the only thing these requests have in common is the general feeling that we have to respond if they come from friends or colleagues.

Fact: *You don't have to respond in the way they ask.*

You might, for instance, answer the manuscript request in many different ways:

1a. *No.*

1b. *I'm really excited that you've written a book, but I don't feel qualified to give an opinion.*

1c. *I'd like to do it, but I don't have time to do the kind of job that would satisfy me.*

1d. *I don't have the time now, but I'd be glad to do it next January, if that would be useful.*

1e. *I think I'm too close to you to give an honest opinion. You might ask Jack, or Lizzie.*

1f. *I can give you my opinion of the outline, and perhaps a sample chapter, but not the whole book.*

1g. *When a manuscript is written in pencil, on yellow paper, I have a hard time reading it without getting angry because my eyes hurt. If you get it typed, I'd be glad to read it.*

1h. *Do you remember how hurt you were when I told you what I really thought of your previous manuscript? I'd rather remain your friend, so the answer is "no."*

1i. *What do you think of the manuscript?*

Fact: *You don't even have to respond at all.*

"But I Just Had to Respond." Looking at some item in this example, you might say, "Oh, I could *never* say that, especially to a friend." Such lack of choice freezes you into a narrow range of options based on illusions, assumptions, fear, or anxiety.

Fact: *Choice among feedback responses empowers you.*

Fact: *Choice among feedback responses empowers the person to whom you respond.*

You can see how choice empowers both you and your friends from the following dialogue that resulted when Jerry chose not to respond to the request as given.

Jerry: What do *you* think of the manuscript?

Joe: Well, um, actually, I don't think it's really ready to show to anyone.

Jerry: Then what do you really want from me?

Joe: I guess I need a little encouragement to make another draft.

Jerry: Well, I don't know if you should make another draft or not. For me, I usually have to go through about three drafts before it's worth showing to anyone.

Joe: Really? But you're such an experienced writer.

Jerry: Yes, and part of my experience tells me that if I ask for feedback too soon, I get discouraged by people's reactions to my rough draft.

Joe: Gee, I never thought of that. Thanks.

Joe eventually redrafted the book and published it, yet Jerry never responded to his direct request for feedback. Instead, he asked Joe about himself and gave him information about his own writing experience. He exercised his choice about how to respond, and gave Joe the choice of how to deal with that response.

Know Your Choices. If you're going to deal effectively with so many collegial or friendly requests for feedback, you'll have to increase your capacity to choose freely. To do that, you must practice making the choice of whether or not to engage the other person, and if so, how to engage him.

Feedback is not something that has to come out of your mouth, or has to be held in. If it *does* come out, it doesn't have to come out the particular *way* you said it. There are always choices, though we may be cowardly and pretend there are not. Teach yourself to notice when you say things like, "I just had to respond," or "Anyone would have said what I did."

Get a lot of practice. Speak up when you usually keep quiet. Keep quiet when you usually speak up. Say something different from what you usually say. Any one particular choice is not so important, so it's okay to make mistakes.

Just by preparing to make a choice, you may learn something important about yourself and your relationship, without even taking the next step of engaging with that other live person. If your choices are conscious, you don't have to give feedback to benefit.

Fact: *The less you actually feed back, the more you get out of it.*

The Decision to Respond to a Request for Feedback. The first step in responding to a request for feedback is to see that you always have a choice whether or not to respond. Here are some of the things you might think about.

1. *Is there really some unfinished business between me and the other person?* You are likely to find that the closer you are to someone, the more the unfinished business.

2. *What is the business, really?* Once again, when you're close, it's more likely that one piece of business is all tangled with another.

3. *What is my current investment in exploring that business?* You'll probably have lots of unfinished business, with lots

of people, so it helps to give them some priority or payoff rating.

4. *Does this request really address our unfinished business, or is it about something else?* If it's about something else, you'll only confuse the situation by tying the two things together.

Once you've honestly considered these questions, you're ready to tackle the question, "Why don't I tell them?"

Experiences

1. Think of a time when a close colleague asked for your honest opinion, then got upset when you gave it. List at least three other ways you could have handled the request.

2. Can you remember a time when your manager offered you some feedback about something in your personal life? If so, write down some of your reactions to the feedback.

3. Can you think of some time when you offered such personal feedback to someone over whom you held authority? Do you know how they reacted? How else might you have handled the situation? What's the difference between this experience and the previous one?

4. It is wise to keep coming back to the concept of rules for commenting when looking at choices for feedback, since all of us learned early some do's and don'ts, though not necessarily the same ones. Here's an experience you can try with your work group.

Make up a number of slips of paper, each of which has on it a rule about commenting, such as,

- *If you can't say something nice, don't say anything at all.*
- *Say the good part first (even if you have to make it up), then tell them the truth (the bad stuff).*
- *Give them the bad news first.*
- *Don't pussy-foot around.*
- *Play dumb.*
- *Never let them know how you really feel.*

(You might use the same rules you've found in a previous experience.) Each person draws a slip out of a hat, not showing the others, then you conduct 5 minutes of one of your ordinary meetings with everyone following their secret rule about commenting. If you can stand another round, throw the slips back in the hat and do it again. Discuss what you learned about the way you customarily give each other feedback.

Chapter 5
The Fear of Giving
Feedback

*Kickin' someone when
they're down sometimes
is the only way to make
them get up.*

We've now spent two chapters warning you to be careful about choosing to give feedback. That's because the most common mistake is giving feedback when you shouldn't. The next most common mistake, however, is not offering feedback when you should, as the following examples illustrate.

Why Don't You Tell Them?

Dear Edie:

Wormwood and I have shared an office for 13 years. He's always been a good colleague, a warm and wonderful man in every way — except one. Even after 13 years, he's still an enthusiastic team member — which is where the trouble starts. He's so eager to read his mail that he strips off the envelopes and flings them at the wastebasket — and usually misses. Then he gets so involved in the letters that he doesn't notice, and he leaves the envelopes lying around for me to pick up. I have a bad back, and besides, shredded envelopes annoy me no end, especially after 13 years. What should I do?

\- BROKEN BACK, BROKEN BOW, NEBRASKA

Dear Broken:

Why don't you tell him?

Dear Jerry:

I have a terrific job as a systems analyst. I make good money, the work is interesting and important, and I like my co-workers. My problem is my boss. She's a great boss except that whenever we have a meeting, at the end of the meeting she pats me on the derriere and calls me "Sweetie." I detest the name, and I especially can't stand her touching me, particularly on my bottom. How can I stop her?

\- NOT SO SWEET, SWEETWATER, OKLAHOMA

Dear Not So,

Why don't you tell her?

Dear Charlie:

Rutherford and Wilma are my co-workers and best friends, but one problem keeps gnawing at me. We share dozens of interests, especially object-oriented programming, Macintosh internals, and adaptive network software. They are kind, loyal, and generous, and are always there when I need them. My problem is that though I think they're terrific, they don't seem to know how I feel. How can I make them realize that I feel so wonderful about them?

\- GNAWED BY ANXIETY, GNAW BONE, INDIANA

Dear Gnawed,

Why don't you tell them?

You may think that the humorous examples given in the three letters above are exaggerations if not complete fictions. Truth be told, we didn't receive them in the form of letters, but as face-to-face requests from clients. Also, we must confess that we've disguised a few of the details, to protect client confidentiality. And just to wrap it up, here's a case that in one form or another, Charlie, Jerry, and Edie have heard at least a hundred times.

Dear Charlie,

I am a department head in a big hospital. I am in danger of losing my best radiologist because of a stupid thing. She shares a locker with a woman from Iran whose clothes not only smell but are making everything else in the locker smell. The radiologist refuses to say anything about it and has told me she is going to quit unless I do something about it. I am reluctant to say anything for fear of an EEO complaint. What should I do?

Dear Depot Head,

Why don't you tell her?

Dear Charlie,

Why don't I tell who?

The Cost of Telling Them

It's not that these people are *unable* to offer feedback. The same person who blurts out feedback to any stranger with only the slightest provocation sometimes goes mute toward a dear friend over some really important matter.

The most frequent case is the manager who can't tell an employee something that's part of that manager's job to tell. We probably could run a specialty consulting business on just one question: "I have this employee who keeps doing so-and-so that's unacceptable, and I've put off his semi-annual performance appraisal for four months now because I don't know what to do about it. What should I do?"

This is such a delicate matter that we seldom actually answer by asking, "Why don't you tell her?" To understand the delicacy of the situation, try to recall a time when someone asked you, "Why don't you tell him?" Do you remember the emotional panic, followed by a rapid sequence of internal responses?

First there was the rush of perfectly good reasons for not telling him, followed immediately by the feeling that such a direct approach would be cheating, like collecting the $200 without passing Go. Then you resented the person making the suggestion, with all its implied superiority. Doesn't she appreciate what terrible things the other person might do if we actually told him, straight out?

Fact: *You can't effectively give emotionally difficult feedback, unless you understand the source of your difficult emotions.*

Let's see where some of this emotional cost originates.

Do You Want to Risk Finding Out How They Feel?

First of all, in order to justify the emotional cost of talking directly to someone, there has to be some payoff that will compensate for the risk. Where is the payoff for "telling him?" Will you succeed in influencing the other person in the way you would like? Experience tells us that's not likely. Perhaps you'll feel better when you "get it off your chest." That's possible, but not probable.

Recall some of your experiences of telling someone directly whatever you were feeling, thinking, or believing about her. The other person always responds, one way or another. She may breathe easier or momentarily catch her breath. She may blush, stammer, sigh with relief, radiate with interest, bristle with anger, or glow with love.

You will immediately perceive any misunderstandings or distortions. You will notice whether she seeks clarification or changes the subject. You will see whether the comments are welcomed or rejected. And you will suddenly know more about her investment in you, as well as her preferred level of relationship:

Manager: Several people have complained to me about the messiness in your cubicle.

Employee: That's just like you, to cite anonymous "people." You never have the courage to stand behind your own opinion as your own. Frankly, if you had enough courage to ask me on your own behalf, I'd clean up my cube in a minute.

In short, you want to tell her because you want to improve your relationship with her. But her response creates an opportunity for you to discover something about that relationship. Maybe what you'll find out is that she doesn't like you as much as you like her.

Fact: *If you want to tell them so they'll like you, what keeps you from telling them is the same emotion, the fear of not being liked. That's one reason you feel so paralyzed.*

Do You Want to Get Involved?

But suppose this fear is not realized, and she does like you? What are the chances that you'll want the feedback you get in return for your direct feedback?

What you discover from giving feedback will be important, but not necessarily relevant to anything you're concerned with right now. If her response will divert you from a more important task, relationship, or activity, isn't it best not to say anything?

When you give someone feedback, you will learn about her. If you don't really care or dare to know more about her, why bother starting an interaction by giving feedback?

Manager: "For some time now, you've been careless with your work. You don't seem to have your mind here, and you're not doing yourself any good."

Employee: "I've tried not to let it interfere with my work, but my twin daughters both have leukemia. I'm scheduled to give them a bone marrow transplant next month, and I only hope it will be in time."

Surprises like this are enough reason for not risking feedback. Yet sometimes, you know in advance what he'll say when you tell him. If you already feel so sure of someone's response that you won't take the time to understand it, why waste time saying something that will produce the response?

Everyone knows that raising sticky issues or engaging in conflict with someone increases the likelihood of future human contacts between you. It's not the only way, of course, and it's not a very good way. Wouldn't it be foolish to get involved in this complex way if you lack any strong desire to see someone again?

Fact: *You often won't tell them because you fear getting involved.*

Do You Want to Get Information?

You may want to get involved, but only if the other person changes.

Fact: *"Telling them" can be a way to play, "If one of us is going to change, why don't you go first?"*

By starting the "telling them" game, you can first see if it will be lethal. But not everybody is willing to play that game, so if you play "telling them," you may wind up learning something about yourself:

Manager: "I have a report from the personnel office that your time sheets are three months behind."

Employee: "I know. They're in that pile on your desk." (This is referred to as "boomerang feedback.")

You think you know how both of you will react in the feedback situation, but are your hunches on target? By "telling them," you subject your speculations to a field test, allowing you to explore discrepancies between your self-concept and what you experience in the interaction. Do you want to know about your discrepancies?

Fact: *You may avoid direct feedback because you fear learning the truth about yourself.*

"Telling them" exposes you to the possibility of surprise-and therefore to the possibility of change. By definition, discovery is not predictable. Although you set out to change the other person, you might wind up changing yourself, which is not too safe. Do you want to change?

Fact: *You may avoid direct feedback because you fear change.*

What Are You Up To?

But suppose you were sure you wouldn't change. "Why don't you tell them?" Turn the question around. "Why *do* you tell them?" Why take the time, energy, and risk to give another person feedback about your reaction to him? What is it that you want to do, now that you're aware of the possibility of such a conversation?

As we've seen, many people who offer feedback say they are doing it for the other person. "Growing" other people is a frustrating and often fruitless pursuit.

Fact: *The less investment you have in changing the other person, the greater likelihood that each of you may grow.*

This paradoxical fact is one good reason for letting go of the fantasy that you can change the other person.

Being realistic about it, you might admit your inherent selfishness and substitute the goal of exploring and discovering something new about yourself. Being even more realistic, it takes a mighty effort to admit you're doing something for yourself. It's so tempting to revert to the pretense that you're giving them feedback "for their own good."

Fact: *You avoid telling them out of fear of being known.*

Lack of Experience

We know from Satir's Interaction Model that such emotional reactions tell us that something has touched one of our survival rules. Somewhere, deep inside, there's a survival rule like one of these:

- *If I tell them, they won't love me; then they'll leave me; then I'll die.*
- *If I talk directly, they'll never do what I want.*

- *If I mention this, there will be a conflict, and I can't deal with conflict.*

- *I'm lucky to have what little I have, and I might lose it if I ask for more.*

- *If I talk openly, then they'll find out what I'm really like, and that would be terrible.*

- *If I tell them, then we'll get closer, and when I get close to someone, I get hurt.*

Such survival rules are much more likely to be activated if our self esteem is low, but almost everybody can be surprised to find themselves morbidly afraid of saying some simple thing to someone close to us. One of the reasons we're easily frightened is a rule something like this:

Whatever I do, I must do perfectly.

Even after we get in touch with our own motives, it's still difficult to use feedback effectively. You must develop a strategy for being secure enough to tolerate the unpredictability, without concealing your true purposes. To get full benefit, you must learn to pay attention and be capable of perceiving what's actually going on. Let's face it, giving feedback is not a simple thing to do. At least, that's been our experience in the past.

A lot of our fear of telling them comes from inexperience, or rather experience at giving feedback poorly and then getting a poor result. But getting a poor result is such a terrible experience only if we have a perfection rule. And where did we get such a rule? From our parents, when they were so big and we were so little that we thought that they were perfect. Now, as an adult, don't you think that's a bit contrary to the facts of life?

Fact: *Nobody's perfect.*

Fact: *Feedback is a lot easier to give if you don't have to be perfect.*

Fact: *Feedback's not so hard to give after all.*

Experiences

1. Try to recall a time when someone asked you, "Why don't you tell her?" Do you remember the emotional panic, followed by a rapid sequence of internal responses? What did you do with that feedback?

2. When someone turns your critical feedback around (like the employee whose boss forgot to turn in the time sheets), you've experienced what the Australians call "boomerang feedback." Give an example of a time when you managed to boomerang someone who was criticizing you. Give a second example of a time when someone managed to boomerang you. What did the two cases have in common?

3. Identify one of your survival rules that you invoke when you contemplate giving feedback, such as,

- *If I mention this, there will be a conflict, and I can't deal with conflict.*

Use a "partner" to help you take your rule to its ultimate, in a series of steps, as we did previously, by asking your partner, at each step, "And then what would happen?" For example:

- *If I mention this, there will be a conflict, and I can't deal with conflict.*

And if you didn't deal with the conflict, then what would happen?

- *Then I'd have to run away.*

And if you ran away, then what would happen?

- *Then I'd be all alone.*

And if you were all alone, then what would happen?

- *Then I'd go crazy.*

And if you went crazy, then what would happen?

- *Then I'd die.*

Part 3

Receiving Feedback

The Giver's Fantasy: *If feedback has all the correct ingredients in its delivery — clear, specific, timed right, non-judgmental, and speaks only to behavior — it will be accepted as given.*

The Giver's Fantasy has, for years, been offered in communication training workshops as a check-list for causing predictable behavior in another person. Despite all this careful preparation, the receivers still make the interpretations they wish. Even so, because of their childhood experience, many receivers share the Giver's Fantasy, which on their side becomes:

The Receiver's Fantasy: *The receiver is controlled by the giver's feedback.*

In this chapter, however, we'll see that the facts are quite different. Whatever receivers do with the feedback is totally within their control. They can reject all of it, or any part of it, swallow it whole or spit it out, distort it, adore it, hate it, forget it, or remember it forever. This is The Receiver's Fact, with one important addition:

The Receiver's Fact: *The receiver is totally in control of feedback, but the control is not necessarily conscious.*

It's the "not necessarily conscious" that makes it hard for us to believe that we are totally in control, for we are often not conscious that we are in control. And until there is a conscious exchange between the receiver and the giver, what happened to the feedback will always be a mystery.

Chapter 6
Why Feedback Is Mysterious

> *There's a little boy a'sleepin' in many a grown man you'd call sensible.*

Feedback is supposed to be informative, but much of the time it's simply mysterious. Working with one of his clients, Charlie saw the following brief interaction between Sue and Sam:

Sue: "Someone has to get the client file."

Sam: "I'm willing to do it."

Sue: (sounding hurt) "If you're going to feel that way about it,

I'll do it myself!"

At this moment, everyone in the room grew silent. Charlie looked at Sue and raised both eyebrows. "What's happening for you?" he inquired.

Sue's eyes misted over. "I...I don't know," she stumbled. "It just came out of me."

It Just Came Out We've all had that experience, when feedback "just came out." In the light of such experiences, it's hard to believe that we really do have choices. Yet in any interaction, we have many choices, including whether to respond, when to respond, what to respond to, and how to respond.

Yet these choices are not meaningful when things "just come out" of our mouths. In order to take advantage of our choices, we need to examine what goes on between the time Sam says, "I'm willing to do it," and Sue screams, "If you're going to feel that way about it, I'll do it myself." It only takes a fraction of a second to respond, but many things are going on inside Sue's head.

Is there any wonder that people have so much trouble understanding each other, or even themselves? If you examine many interactions, such as this one between Sam and Sue, you'll discover that there are a number of reasons why feedback can be so confusing:

Different Perceptions We may be similar, but in the end, we are different people, so our perceptions differ. We extract different information from the same situation, so that, generally, what I send is not what you receive, as in the following three examples:

1. "You can't call me a liar!" (I said you made a mistake.)

2. "You told me to send him that report." (I told you that he didn't have a copy of the report.)

3. "Why didn't you tell me it was due on Thursday?" (I told you.)

Different Time We can get confused when part of the feedback doesn't refer to the present, but to the past or future, as in these examples:

1. "You used to give me a personal report after every meeting." *(past)*

2. "You might not get that job done on time." *(future)*

3. "I never could deal with angry people, and you're going to get angry if I tell you." *(past and future)*

Different Place We may be mystified because part of the feedback refers to some other context, as in these examples:

1. "You said we should have more structure in our committee meetings, so why are you objecting to my agenda?" *(This is not a committee meeting. This is lunch.)*

2. "You drink coffee in my office, so why can't I smoke in your office?" *(First of all, coffee isn't smoke. Second of all, my office is an explosives laboratory.)*

Someone Else We'll also be thrown off center when part of the feedback refers to some other person:

1. "My mother used to point her finger at me when I had been naughty, and you're a woman, too." *(I'm not your mother, I'm the personnel director. In fact, I don't have any children.)*

2. "My brother always lies to me about money, and you have curly hair just like my brother." *(I'm not your brother, I'm your staff assistant.)*

3. "My previous three bosses never fulfilled their promises to me, so obviously you can't be trusted." *(I'm not your previous bosses, I'm your present boss. Actually, though, you do remind me of an employee I once had.)*

Inner Feelings about Myself My feelings about myself have a powerful influence on how I respond. If I feel bad about myself, I may be more critical of things. If I feel good, I may be more inclined to see things in a favorable light. But, if you're unaware of what my feelings are, you're likely to be confused. You might get two different responses to the same report:

1. "You (the receiver) did a good job on this report." *(You may not know it, but I just closed the biggest order of the year, and I feel great.)*

2. "This report is late, sloppy, and full of errors." *(My husband's overdrawn our checking account again, but I don't dare confront him.)*

So which feedback should you believe? Is it a neat, timely, and accurate report? Who knows?

The Receiver's Task All of these confusing factors — different perceptions, different times, different places, or different people, as well as my inner feelings about myself — tend to combine in the most confusing feedback situations. When this happens — as it quite likely did with Sue — something may have triggered a "survival rule," and we've already seen what that does in Satir's Interaction Model.

So many mystifying factors can be discouraging, but keep in mind that once you know about these reasons why feedback is mysterious, you're well down the road to becoming a more capable receiver of feedback.

Experiences

1. Can you recall a recent event when something "just came out?" What did you realize about yourself when this happened? What was another's reaction to you? What other choices could you make at another time?

2. Do you recall any feedback now or in the past when different perceptions, times, places, or persons confused the clarity of the message? How much dust was spread before it was settled? How could it have been settled earlier?

Chapter 7
The Feedback Prevention Law

*Happiness depends more
on how life strikes you
than on what happens.*

Feedback is always available to us. We can get it from ourselves: the way we're feeling, the climate around us, the songs we're singing, and the sighs we're sighing. It also comes from those around us: what they're saying and not saying to us, and their non-verbal behavior. Consider this interaction between Jerry and Retha:

Jerry: Blah, blah, blah....

Retha: You're babbling!

Jerry: Blah, blah, blah....

Retha may wonder how Jerry can be unaware of her clear feedback, but the Law of Intake says that one of Jerry's choices — his very first choice — is to be *unaware* that feedback is present. Part of being unaware is not a choice, but part of it is. If you're reading this book, you've made a choice to be more aware of feedback.

If Jerry is *unaware* that feedback is present, his other choices become meaningless, so the logical first step in learning to use feedback is to learn to be *aware* of feedback. In our experience, however, *most* feedback never passes the awareness phase. That's why we'll use this chapter to examine why *anyone* could be unaware of clear feedback. Let's start with the story of Ramon, a Mexican executive who came to the United States for residential management training at Harvard University.

Ramon Does His Laundry Ramon had never been away from Mexico before, except on business trips where he lived in hotels. Being a Mexican male of an upper middle-class family, Ramon had never had the problem of doing laundry. His laundry had always been somehow magically taken away dirty and returned clean a few hours later.

After one week in the Harvard dormitory, Ramon found that the laundry was not disappearing and reappearing. In fact, it was accumulating, and he had nothing clean to wear. He discussed this problem with his roommate, who told him that he should go downstairs to the basement where there were machines to wash his clothes. To be extra helpful, the roommate gave him some change and a bottle of liquid detergent.

When Ramon got downstairs, however, he saw that there were *two* machines, and — not having ever been concerned with laundry — he had no idea which one to use. One machine looked rather old and more heavily used, so he decided to use the newer machine to do a better job. Consequently, he put his laundry in the *dryer,* poured in a generous quantity of liquid detergent, inserted his coins, and started the dryer, thinking that this was going to wash his clothes.

When Ramon came back an hour later to retrieve the clothes, he noticed that they were caked with blue soap that had been baked into the material. Somehow, this blueness didn't seem right. Perhaps the clothes were not sufficiently washed, he thought. He put them back in the dryer, added more soap, put in some more money, and ran the dryer again.

When he retrieved his clothes the second time, they looked even worse. Perhaps this was as good as the machine could wash them, he thought. He took the clothes upstairs, folded them, and put them away.

After five days of wearing blue underwear, Ramon's skin was peeling off. He was becoming desperate, itching the hours away in long lectures on economic decision making and strategic planning. He decided that something was wrong with his clothes and that he had to wash them again.

This time, however, when he got downstairs the new washing machine (which we know was actually the dryer) was filled with somebody else's clothes. He was very hesitant to use the old machine, but he desperately needed clean clothes. He decided that he had better risk it. He put the clothes in the old machine, added some detergent, inserted his coins, turned on the machine, and went away.

When Ramon returned an hour later, he saw bubbles pouring out of the machine all over the floor. Ramon knew that he had made some kind of mistake. When he opened the machine, he found his clothes were still wet. He thought, "Oh, I knew this was an old machine and wouldn't work very well. It didn't even dry my clothes."

He put the clothes in the dryer (which he still thought was the washer) to wash them again. He had no more detergent, so he just thought he would run them through in order for this superior machine to rinse them out and dry them. Sure enough, when they came out, they were dry and clean, further confirming his belief that the "new washer" was better.

Later in the week, he asked his roommate how to get more detergent, and the roommate became suspicious. Only then did Ramon finally learn the difference between a washer and a dryer.

Do More of the Same Like Ramon, we are most likely to be unaware of feedback when we find ourselves in a new situation—precisely the situation where we need to learn the most.

Like Ramon, when we try to solve a problem and it doesn't work, most of us simply try to do *more of the same thing.* Ramon not only washed the clothes again, he used even more detergent than the previous time.

We laugh at Ramon because our own follies are equally silly:

When Charlotte is criticized by her boss for not speaking up in meetings, she responds by going deeper into her shell.

When any of his employees behaves badly, Frank responds with more abusive, demeaning remarks.

When Gilda's friends walk away from her in the cafeteria, Gilda responds by talking louder and faster.

How is it possible for Ramon, Charlotte, Frank, and Gilda to be so stupid? How is it possible for *us* to be so stupid?

Our Laws of the World Each of us has an elaborate set of laws, not always conscious, of how the world works. These laws affect the *interpretation* step in Satir's interaction model. For instance, Charlotte believes that her boss is trying to catch her making mistakes, so he can embarrass her in front of her coworkers. When her boss calls on her to draw out the intelligence he knows she possesses, Charlotte's "law" tells her she must hide.

These "laws" derive from our *survival rules.* For instance, Frank believes that people are essentially bad, so that without continued correction, they will become worthless employees.

These laws often take the form of *rules about commenting*. Gilda believes that people will not like her unless she can hold their attention by saying many clever things. Therefore, she never comments on anything without trying to be clever.

Charlotte and Frank and Gilda have acquired these "laws" through a lifetime of painful mistakes.

When Charlotte first came to the United States, she was ridiculed by her classmates and one of her teachers because of her Swedish accent.

Frank's father beat him regularly, accompanied by verbal abuse. But he always said, after beating him, "I only did this so you'll grow up to be a good citizen."

Gilda's heart was broken when she lost her first steady boyfriend. He told her that his new girlfriend was "much more interesting." He was talking about looser morals, but Gilda thought he meant her conversational style.

The Law of Conservation of Laws In order to persist in such "stupid" behavior, we have to ignore what seems to be "obvious" feedback. Ramon's case is easiest to analyze because the feedback is from a machine, not a person. The feedback is obvious to us, because we already know the difference between a washer and a dryer.

It wasn't obvious to Ramon because he came from a different culture, with different laws about laundry. As he received each new piece of feedback, Ramon used it to confirm his laws, not to challenge them. It's exactly the same in the other cases.

The boss's criticism for not speaking up is "proof" to Charlotte that she needs to hide herself more effectively from his attention.

An employee's crashing the computer is "proof" to Frank that the previous abuse wasn't sufficiently severe.

Gilda's departing audience is proof that she's not talking sufficiently loud or fast.

This, then, is the *Law of Conservation of Laws:*

When the data and their model don't match, most people discard the data.

At first sight, the Law of Conservation of Laws may look stupid, but it's a sensible way to behave – when seen from the inside. If these laws cost us so much pain and misery to acquire, does it make sense to let go of them just because of one piece of feedback that they're not working?

Not at all. It makes more sense to develop an explanation of what went wrong in this particular instance, thus converting the exception into "proof" of the law.

Although one application of the Law of Conservation of Laws makes good sense, one hundred applications creates a convoluted image of the world that costs us an incredible amount to maintain. But since we have so much invested in our laws, we can't let them go. The Law of Conservation of Laws keeps right on being one of the strongest reasons why *most feedback intended to change other people's behavior is a waste of time.*

The Feedback Prevention Law The Law of Conservation of Laws says we discard data that doesn't fit our view of the world. As if this were not enough protection for us, we go a step further:

We structure our world so we will not receive feedback that threatens our world view.

This is the *Feedback Prevention Law*. It says that we will not even wait to *ignore* feedback, but actively take steps to *prevent* feedback from ever happening in the first place.

Charlotte *always* hides from her boss. She's so afraid of what will happen if she doesn't hide that she has no way of knowing what will actually happen.

Frank *always* abuses his employees when they do something wrong. He's so afraid of what will happen if he doesn't abuse them that he has no way of knowing how they will respond to some other sort of interaction.

Gilda *always* talks a thousand words a minute. She's so afraid of what will happen if she stops talking that she has no way of knowing what will happen if she is sometimes quiet.

The Feedback Prevention Law says that people often structure their lives to avoid feedback in those areas where they could most use it—where their models of the world are inadequate. That's why feedback from other people is even more important than it might otherwise be.

In theory, feedback from others would be the most efficient method of learning. But the Law of Conservation of Laws says that when people do get feedback, they'll interpret it according to their existing models of the world. That's why feedback from other people seldom produces any change.

And that's why we tend to learn, like Ramon, only in *new* situations, which force us out of our usual well-protected world. And that's why, if we want to learn from personal feedback, we have to examine the entire structure of our world, and probably change it in some way.

Experiences

1. Remind yourself of an experience when you knew something was wrong but could not give up your assumptions—like Ramon substituting assumptions of machines being new and old for washer and dryer.

a. What kinds of assumptions blocked you?

b. How did you eventually come to your senses?

c. Can you laugh about your assumptions now? Could you laugh then? What has happened to make the difference, or what hasn't happened so that there's no difference?

d. How recently have you found yourself defying your own perceptions?

2. How might the Feedback Prevention Law apply to you?

a. Identify a situation in which you are aware of your fear of discovering what the feedback is.

b. Ask yourself, "what is the worst thing that I could find out?" What is your reaction to your own worst case scenario?

c. What is the chance that this worst case scenario will actually occur, at this time and in this place?

d. What is the chance that, even if it does occur, you'll be able to deal with it better than you would have in another place at another time?

Chapter 8
Finding People to Give You Feedback

After some folks tell you all they know, they keep on talkin'.

In actual practice, most feedback smashes itself against an elaborate structure designed to prevent feedback. That's why it's more likely that change will be produced by a new context that produces a consistent new pattern of rewards and punishment, along with structural limits on our choices. We're all familiar with the low rated employee who seems totally unresponsive to management feedback, and then takes a new assignment and becomes top rated.

But it's not always convenient to take a new job if we want to become more efficient in our learning. We need to create or find new environments for ourselves with somewhat less disturbance than changing jobs.

But where are these new environments, somewhere over the rainbow, in the Land of Oz? Indeed, Oz was just the kind of environment Dorothy needed, because it wasn't like Kansas. It had a different system of rewards and punishments, and Dorothy was ultimately under the protection of the Good Witch of the North.

The Rainbow Bridge Speaking of The Wizard of Oz, do you remember "Over the Rainbow?" Judy Garland sang that song when she played Dorothy, and sang so well that she became famous. Everywhere she went her audience begged her to sing "Over the Rainbow."

Judy became a famous entertainer by doing one thing very well and very often. People were drawn to her performance and created a relationship with her. For Judy, "Over the Rainbow" started as a performance, but eventually grew into a bridge, a rainbow bridge, connecting her with her fans. When Judy first sang "Over the Rainbow," she didn't know it would make her famous. It's the same way for all of us. Whenever we do a new act, some people like it and others don't, but it constructs a rainbow bridge to those who do. For instance, when little Jimmy was four years old, his mother and father started having violent quarrels over money. Jimmy was too young to understand about money, but he certainly understood quarrels. He didn't like them.

Whenever Mommy and Daddy quarreled, Jimmy got agitated and began to try different acts. These acts had little effect on the quarrels, until one day Mommy and Daddy noticed Jimmy standing on his head on top of the kitchen table. He looked so silly they burst out laughing, totally forgetting their quarrel. Jimmy was pleased to be able to stop quarrels, and the following week he did a repeat performance.

Thirty years later, Jimmy was known to all his colleagues as "the clown." Rather than dismantle the rainbow bridge to his friends, Jimmy embellished his clown act. Jimmy had created a survival rule:

When people start to argue, I must always play the clown.

Just like Judy, Jimmy had become one of his acts. Even when he wanted to be serious, his colleagues interpreted his attempt as a joke, thus reinforcing his survival rule.

Establishing an Environment Through Sorting Over time, people who didn't like to have a clown interrupting every serious situation began to avoid Jimmy. That's not unusual behavior. People who don't like your act tend to avoid you, so you don't see them any more. People who do like your act find a way to keep in contact. After a while, like Jimmy and Judy, you find yourself surrounded by people who like your act and avoided by people who don't. We call this process "sorting."

Sorting is always operating to build each one of us an audience. Through our audience, we—like Judy and Jimmy—will get feedback whether we like it or not. Through that feedback, our model of the world is either reinforced or challenged.

Sorting is a two-way street, involving both you and the sorter. It depends on what you do, but it also depends on what the other people want. People who want to be connected will give you one kind of feedback — the basic function of which is to get or stay connected. People who want to be disconnected will give another kind of feedback — the basic function of which is to change your behavior. If you won't change your behavior, then the disconnectors will simply go away.

Over time, the process of sorting creates an environment that will not provide feedback that leads to change. Every day you remain in this environment, your model of the world gets validated, no matter how inappropriate it might be in other environments. "If my act is so terrible," you ask, "how come my colleagues like it so much?"

What's Needed to Change It's pleasant to be surrounded by friends and admirers, but if you ever get tired of doing "Over the Rainbow" or "The Clown," you have a problem.

You want to create a new act—perhaps to get a new job—but when you stop doing the old act, it's like blowing up the bridge that connects you with the people who are closest to you.

Your fans have to choose how to cope with the loss of a familiar bridge. They may move away from you, search for a new connection, rethink their need for a connection, or continue pleading for the old familiar act. Each of these choices tends to put pressure on you not to change.

When their adored one changes, your fans are forced to change. Perhaps their feedback, their connection, was initially designed to protect them from changing, but it also locks you, the performer, into a million repetitions of "Over the Rainbow." People who are successful in their work may have the hardest time restructuring their world if they want to do something else. An interesting exception was Beverly Sills, the great opera singer. Beverly decided to retire from her singing career so she could manage the opera. It goes without saying that the many devoted fans who regularly used the bridge to her were of an entirely different mind. "Please, Beverly, just one more time," they pleaded. "Come on Beverly, you can come back just for a while, just for us." They couldn't believe that if they pleaded hard enough she wouldn't change her mind, but she didn't. The reason she didn't is instructive to all of us who want to use feedback to build new bridges, rather than shore up the rickety old ones.

Flattering feedback certainly feels wonderful, but it also freezes us in the identity of a moment. Unless we have some "fans" of a different kind, the kind who will support us in the changes we want to make, we're stuck.

Beverly Sills had such a fan, who happened to be her husband. To help her blow the bridges, he gave her a ring inscribed with a magic phrase. And whenever her fans would plead, "Just one more time," Beverly would look down, take a deep breath, and read in a gracious but convincing tone, "I've done that already."

New Environments We have chosen our old environments and been chosen by them to support our old views of the world. To change, we need to change those views, and to do that, we can't keep doing the same acts. We need new environments to take away all the flattery from our former "fans." If they are still around, our own changes will tend to force them to change. To protect their views of the world, they'll react with highly critical feedback.

Even without the critical feedback, feedback from new environments tends to be puzzling, like Ramon's encounters with the dryer. When we try something new, we feel awkward and incompetent. We'd like to hear feedback about how well we are progressing. Instead, we tend to hear feedback on where we are, which at first is not very close to where we want to be.

In short, just when you need feedback the most, it's most likely to be most critical, most puzzling, and not at all what you need to hear. So what can you do to make the environment more amenable to our receiving feedback? There are two crucial parts to such an environment, the right people and the right atmosphere.

The Right People Your eventual goal is to learn to deal more productively with the people who are close to you, such as your coworkers. But such people may be committed either to changing you or keeping you the same. In order to practice for the real thing, you can start by finding some people who are not too close. After you've learned

learned a few things, you can bring them back to the more familiar environment and see what happens.

You will feel less defensive around someone who doesn't hold an important position in your life. Both parties are less likely to be hurt, or, if hurt, to recover quickly.

The more central persons in your life take great risks when they offer you feedback. Strangers will often express themselves to you more openly, because they have less to fear if you decide to retaliate. "Even your best friends won't tell you" should more accurately be expressed as "Especially your best friends won't tell you."

Of course, being a stranger is not the only qualification a person needs to be chosen for effective feedback. They also need to feel good enough about themselves to accept your differences. With that combination, you're off on the right foot. All you need now is to set the right environment.

Experiences

1. Is there something about you that you feel is different and not valued, so you have been reluctant to share that part of you? If you were to share that with someone, who would it be? Go for it!

2. If you share the different part of you and get the familiar, undervalued reaction, do you have any new ways of coping with it, so that you can still value your difference? What are they? What would you like to do about them? Do it!

3. If you were to set a date, place, and time to get feedback from a very important person in your life, when would it be, where would it be, and how would you ask him for what kinds of feedback?

Chapter 9
Asking for Feedback

*A person who can't take
a word of criticism hears
it the most.*

Barbara: Why do you look so mad?

Ken: Because you haven't told me you like my work.

Barbara: I like your work.

Ken: Doesn't count.

Barbara: Why not?

Ken: Because I had to ask.

Feedback Is Life Total lack of feedback induces death. This isn't really an observation, but a definition of death — or of life. To live means to interact with an environment. Isolating a living being from its environment does indeed induce death, from suffocation, thirst, starvation.

But why would we die from lack of information? Because we need air, water, and food (and for some members of the species, sex), we are built to get information and use it to obtain those essentials. Feedback, which originally serves as a means to obtaining essential physical items from the environment, eventually becomes an essential item itself. Personal feedback that reassures us that we are alive comes to us in many different forms. It doesn't all come from other people — in fact, for some that is the last resort.

Many people arrange to get the feedback they need (or all that is available to them) from animals (a dog licks their hand), from hobbies (a cook knows how good the soup is), from nature (a garden that grows), or even from machines (a computer program that works, or a biofeedback machine that monitors blood pressure). Perhaps our concept of asking for feedback is limited.

Our addiction to a diet of feedback information makes us suckers for anything that even vaguely resembles feedback, including all sorts of erroneous, irrelevant, and self-serving information given to us by other people. The gambling industry shows how much people will pay for anything slightly resembling feedback.

Why Not Ask For It? This is a chapter on asking for feedback. In view of the essential nature of feedback, the chapter should be one sentence long:

If you want feedback, ask for it.

The only thing wrong with such a chapter is that it wouldn't work. The real work of this chapter is to answer the question,

If feedback is so essential, why are we so reluctant to ask for it? In some sense, the answer is easy. We are so reluctant to ask for feedback because it is so essential. To understand this paradox, consider the following story.

Hamlin's Feedback Sharon was Hamlin's boss. She thought that Hamlin could use some training in human interaction skills, but she didn't have time to train him herself, so she sent him to one of our workshops. When he returned, Sharon asked him about his workshop experience. "It was wonderful," he said.

Sharon wanted something more specific. "In what ways was it wonderful, Hamlin?" she asked.

"Well, they put us in these small groups and then they asked each of us to take as much time as we want to say whatever was on our mind."

"That sounds wonderful, Hamlin."

"And you know what they said after that?"

"What, Hamlin?"

"They said, 'Do you have anything else you want to say?'"

Sharon smiled. "That sounds like a terrific idea."

"Then, why can't we do that in this office?"

Time as Feedback Hamlin's feedback, of course, tells Sharon something about Sharon. It tells Sharon that she may not be practicing what she preaches. The things she can easily teach the trainers to build into their program may be quite difficult for her to build into the way she manages her group.

But Hamlin's feedback also tells Sharon something about Hamlin. In this case, it told her that Hamlin wasn't getting all the feedback he needed at work. His plea is the most common form of request for feedback, especially of workers to their managers. "Give me some of your time."

Sometimes, the manager responds with bewilderment. "But I'm giving you guys at least half of my time." To this, the employee silently replies, "Yes, but that's for your things. What about my things?"

Feedback is such an essential ingredient of life that we are unable to spend time in the presence of another person without exchanging feedback at phenomenal rates. For that reason, a request for time can be considered a request for non-specific, life-maintaining feedback.

If you spend time with a person, even saying nothing, you are giving feedback that says, "You are worth enough for me to spend my time with, even doing nothing." And what more do we want from feedback than reassurance that we are worth something?

Everybody needs at least one group that will give them all the time they need. Not everybody has such a group — especially not at work. Sometimes they find it at work, but not with their own work group. Their managers wonder why they've always manufactured an excuse to be with some other group.

Many people are starving for just this kind of reassuring feedback. They are so starved that they are afraid to ask for feedback, for fear of a refusal. If they don't make a specific request, they may be allowed to just hang around, receiving "time feedback." They fear that once they call attention to themselves by asking for something, they could wind up being dismissed.

The Struggle to Get Feedback With all the different variants of feedback, asking for feedback is never a simple matter. I can easily fail to understand your request for feedback. Therefore, it's easy to see how your request can fail to produce the desired results — even if you were clear-headed and free of personal motives when you delivered the request.

For my feedback to be effective, you and I first have to determine exactly what you want. This requires agreement and understanding between us and within each of us — both formidable undertakings. To obtain this kind of clarification, we both have to have the ability to give and receive feedback. But if we can actually clarify just what it is you're requesting, you probably don't need feedback in the first place. For instance, Ken and Barbara's interaction might have gone differently:

Barbara: Why do you look so mad?

Ken: Because you haven't told me if you like my work.

Barbara: Just exactly what do you want from me?

Ken: I guess I'm feeling rather hurt and vulnerable.

Barbara: Yes, I guess you do look hurt and vulnerable. So what would you like from me?

Ken: I guess I just wanted to know that you knew I was hurt and vulnerable.

Because they have the ability to clarify what they want, by the time they've clarified the request, they've already satisfied the need.

So, there are two more reasons why people don't ask for feedback:

If you really are capable of asking for the particular feedback, 7

you may not need it—you may already have it.

By the time your request is clarified, your need is probably satisfied.

In other words, it's not so much the feedback that counts, but the struggle to get it—not the feedback, but the feed-ing-back.

Why Successful People Don't Seek Feedback Rereading this chapter, Charlie remarked that people often ask him, "If feedback is so important, why is it that most successful people don't often seek feedback? In fact, why do they do things that make feedback difficult?"

We're not sure exactly what is meant by "successful," but we assume it means something like making productive, creative use of one's natural endowments, and a general state of happiness and well-being. If that's the case, the answers should by this time be obvious.

In the first place, successful people don't often seek feedback because they know how to find it all around them. That's one of the skills that has made them successful. In the second place, the things successful people do which "make feedback difficult" also ensure that the feedback they do receive is highly significant. They carefully choose the people they ask, they ensure that the atmosphere is right, and they take great pains to clarify what it is they're really asking for.

And finally, successful people usually have high self-esteem. They are okay with themselves and others, and don't need constant reassurance from the outside that they are okay. Indeed, we might apply the *Foot in Mouth Law* to the person who asked this question in the first place.

We can start with their question, "If feedback is so important, why is it that most successful people don't often seek feedback? In fact, why do they do things that make feedback difficult?" If we translate this by the *Foot in Mouth Law*, which says my question is really about myself, we get this question.

"If feedback is so important, why is it that most successful people don't often seek feedback from me? In fact, why do they do things that make it difficult for me to give them feedback?"

This question sounds a lot like a rather indirect request for reassuring feedback.

Pseudo-requests and Pseudo-feedback Paradoxically, neither the most nor the least successful people seem to spend much time asking for feedback. Their reasons, however, are entirely opposite. Successful people are not hunting for feedback because they're relatively sure they're okay. Unsuccessful people don't seek feedback because they are so sure they are not okay that they don't dare ask for information about themselves.

When my self-esteem is low, but I do manage to ask for feedback, I often do it in manipulative, convoluted ways that guarantee that I won't get any real information. I make every occasion for feedback into a matter of survival, because I am operating out of my survival rules, not out of a felt need for real information. Here's an example:

1. "Didn't you think that some of the examples in my lecture were not too far off target?"

This kind of manipulative "pseudo-asking" limits the amount of real feedback others can give me — that's why I do it. If they do give me anything, it might better be called "pseudo-feedback", because it is not really them telling me anything. Instead, it's them repeating what I have told them to say. And, when they do tell me, I won't believe them because I recognize it as my idea in the first place.

And because I am responding to my inner survival needs rather than the here and now situation, I tend to construct my moments of truth in the wrong place, at the wrong time, for the wrong reason.

2. "If you really think I'm your most valuable employee, you won't get angry when I call you out of a personnel review to ask if you really think I'm a more valuable employee than the one you're reviewing."

When I request feedback in this way, I'm perfectly protected from getting any information I'm afraid to hear. If you don't get angry, then you really do think I'm your most valuable employee. If you do get angry, it's not because you don't value me, but only because you were interrupted in the middle of a delicate meeting, or because you're afraid the other person will find out that they're less valued.

Here are a few more examples of this form of request for feedback that is actually guaranteed to get no feedback at all. Do they sound familiar?

3. "If you're really an effective public speaker, you'll be smooth and unruffled when I interrupt your discourse to tell you that there's been a long history of suicide in my family, and that your lecture just happened to bring back all my suicidal yearnings."

4. "If you're really a qualified supervisor, you'll come up with a perfect response when I break into a meeting with a client and tell you that you screwed up last month's report to another client."

The curious thing is that people with low-self esteem are not actually reassured by this kind of feedback, or any kind of feedback. Their low self-worth comes from deep inside, and cannot be touched from the outside. Often, they construct situations that guarantee they will receive feedback to confirm their low self worth, as in this example:

Ken: I know you hate me, so why don't you tell me you hate me.

Jim: I don't hate you, I just intensely dislike what you're doing.

Ken: Look, I hate me, other people hate me, and you say you dislike what I'm doing, which in my book is the same as hating me.

Jim: Okay then, if that's the way you think, I hate you.

Ken: You really know how to hurt a guy.

Jim: Now I know why I hate you.

For a feedback request to work, there must first be a connection between the people involved. If a request for feedback comes at the wrong time, the wrong place, or on the wrong subject, it may be seen as manipulative, which will tend to destroy the needed connection.

Low self-esteem people, by their convoluted requests for feedback, tend to destroy the connections they need to rebuild their self-worth. Observing the withdrawal of other people, they falsely conclude that they must not ask for feedback. In extreme cases, this vicious cycle leads to withdrawal and depression.

The way out of this life-denying cycle is to learn how to ask for feedback from the right people, at the right time, in the right place, on the right subject. Once they begin to develop that skill, people are rewarded with the kind of feedback that makes human life so marvelous.

Experiences

1. Is there someone in your work who is not giving you the time you want from her? What feedback message are you getting from her unavailability? Have you checked that out? What would you have to do to get her to give you the time? If that doesn't seem possible, is there someone else who can give you the time?

2. Is there someone in your work who you think wants time from you, but you're not giving it to him? What feedback message are you giving him by your unavailability? Have you checked that out? What would you have to do to make the time available to him? If that doesn't seem possible, is there someone else who can give him the time?

3. Choose a "partner." Take turns doing the following, to practice learning to recognize pseudo-feedback:

a. Try asking your partner to give you feedback in such a way that she has no choice but to tell you exactly what you want to hear.

b. If the partner doesn't say exactly what you want, reshape your request to give her fewer choices.

c. Repeat until you get the exact feedback you want, or until you both give up in laughter or disgust.

d. Discuss what insights this gave you into your habitual ways of asking for feedback, and her habitual ways of responding.

Chapter 10
What Aren't They Saying?

> *A good friend is one who tells you your faults in private.*

Voice From Back of Auditorium: I can't hear you back here.

Jerry: (moves closer to the microphone) Is this better?

Voice From Back of Auditorium: Yes, thank you.

Jerry: Thank you for telling me.

Applying the Interaction Model Sometimes, personal feedback is clear, crisp, and clean. But not often. Whenever someone gives you information about yourself, but you cannot figure out why, remember the stages of Satir's Interaction Model.

Check the various internal stages of both your perception and their response, one by one. Later in the book, we'll apply the interaction model to study and improve how you respond to feedback. In this section, however, we'll start by trying to understand what might be going on inside the other person to make him react to you like that.

Although you are trying to figure out what's going on inside the other person, you must, of course, start with what comes out — or what doesn't come out. Perhaps the hardest feedback to deal with is no feedback at all, when people seem not to be interacting with you.

The Skunk and the Dalmatian A baby skunk and a baby dalmatian puppy were roommates. They were both new hires at the Children's Zoo, and every day after work they discussed their experiences. After a few weeks on the job, the skunk got up the courage to tell the puppy about her problem. "Nobody seems to like me. People seem to be avoiding me wherever I go, and I don't understand why. I've been wrestling with the problem, over and over, ever since I started working, and I just can't figure out why."

The puppy said, "I don't understand why either. I don't have that kind of trouble. Nobody seems to be avoiding me, and I have lots of new friends. Yet you and I are just alike — black and white and covered with fur. We laugh, we work hard, we smile, we play, and people are playful when we approach them. Sure, you have that stripe and I have these spots."

"Do you think it could be the stripe?"

"It doesn't seem likely."

"I just don't know what it is I'm doing."

So the skunk remained miserable, trying to find out what it was she was doing and never knowing. Certainly there was feedback all around, but how was the skunk to decipher it?

Of course, this is not really an animal story. It's a people story, in which the people have been disguised as animals for their own protection. Suppose you were the skunk? How would you ever know?

What To Do When Commenting Rules Distort Feedback
Unfortunately, the skunk had a particularly difficult time
understanding her feedback—because she got no feedback at all. She was stymied by a social rule about commenting that prevented her co-workers from saying
anything at all. This social rule says, "don't comment
about anyone's body odors." But if the rule prevents commenting, how are skunks to find out about it?

One way she could approach the problem is to think
about all the widespread rules that people have about not
commenting. Here are a few to consider:

Don't comment about anyone's body odors.

*Don't comment about something the person can't do any-
thing about, like physical impairments or their family members.*

*Don't comment about anything that might embarrass the
person.*

Don't comment about anything sexual.

Don't comment about anything financial.

Don't comment about religion.

Don't show anger (love, grief, joy, any strong feeling, etc.).

*Don't be disrespectful to your elders (to women, to men, to
teachers, to parents, to bosses, etc.)*

This gives you a list of candidates for subject areas that
might be the true source of the feedback.

What To Do When There's No Feedback At All If you feel
that "your best friends aren't telling you," remember the
interaction model and first consider that the problem may
be in your own perception. The skunk kept asking, "What
am *I* doing?" The interaction model would have

reminded her that people don't react to what *you're* doing, but what they're *perceiving*. She might have been more successful asking, "What do they *perceive* that I'm doing?"

Try to sharpen your own perception and extract more information from your surroundings. The key question is:

"What is it I see or hear that makes me believe that I'm getting no feedback?"

Do people avoid you under all circumstances, or do people with stuffy noses seem more friendly? Does it depend on the way the wind is blowing?

Do people really say nothing to you, or are you simply discounting what they say as unimportant?

Are you seeing their non-verbal feedback? Are they holding their noses? Are they turning their backs to you?

Can you convert the non-feedback into feedback? What happens if you say, "Is there something you can't tell me?" and note their non-verbal reaction?

Most important, apply the basic principle of science, which is to change one thing at a time and pay attention to what else changes. If you keep doing the same thing, why do you expect them to change what they're doing?

Displacement of Person Just as confusing as no feedback at all is feedback directed at you that doesn't belong to you. If people have their survival rules triggered, they may need to concoct a defense, and one of the common defenses is to *displace* the feedback. If it's displaced away from you, you may not realize it's really about you. And vice versa. For example, if the rule about commenting does not allow commenting to a particular person, then the feedback may be displaced onto another person.

Hiram: You just kicked me. Why?!

Erma: Cathy just ate my sweetroll.

Hiram: Why didn't you kick Cathy?

Erma: Because she might kick me back!

Displacement can be confusing. Cathy may be confused because she thinks she's not getting any feedback. Hiram is confused because he thinks the feedback could justifiably be directed at him. Like all of us, he feels a little guilty, especially if his self esteem is down. Hiram can probably think of a dozen reasons for Erma to be kicking him, so he might not think to ask.

But *asking* is the only sure way to find out. Even if the feedback *is* directed at Hiram, asking might make it clearer which of the dozen reasons is the true cause. He might also find out why Erma doesn't fear him as much as she does Cathy. So, if the feedback seems at all puzzling, *check it out.*

Displacement of Subject If the rule about commenting does not allow commenting on a particular subject, then the feedback may be displaced onto another subject.

Hiram: You just kicked me. Why?!

Erma: You were pouting.

Hiram: For that you kick me?

Erma: (Silence.) *("I can't tell him he's picking his nose.")*

You can usually identify subject displacement either by the disproportion of the emotion or by the silence that develops when you pursue the disproportion far enough. *Check it out.*

Displacement in Time If the rule about commenting does not allow commenting at a particular time, then the feedback may be displaced to a later time.

Hiram: You just kicked me. Why?!

Erma: You never let me use your terminal.

Hiram: What do you mean? You're using it right now.

Erma: Not *this* time, stupid! When we were working on the Allied project.

Hiram: That was a month ago! Why didn't you kick me then?

Erma: I didn't want the Allied people to think I had a bad temper.

You can often identify time displacement by the key words "never" and "always." Nobody "always" does anything, even you. When someone says you *always* or *never* do something, you can check it out.

For example, you can ask, "When you say I never get my work done on time, I'm really concerned because I think that I'm on time some of the time. Do you mean I don't get it done on certain occasions? Can you be more specific?" Of course, this technique won't *always* work, but it won't always *fail,* either. *Check it out.*

Projection Another common form of defense occurs when the rules about commenting do not allow a person to say certain things about herself. Instead of saying what she feels, she *projects* the feeling onto some convenient bystander, the way a slide projector uses a screen to show an image of the slide within:

Boss: You sound discouraged. Why don't you take a day off?

Bernice: Because I'm not discouraged.

Boss: Well, I'd sure like to take a day off.

Bernice: You should, you sound discouraged.

Boss, being a boss and a man, cannot admit to being more discouraged than his employee, who is a woman, so he uses her as a projection screen. Bernice doesn't take the bait, and Boss just slips out the next day. (Being a boss, he can't admit that he can take a day off without the company suffering.)

Bernice may have made a mistake saying he sounded discouraged, because that may trigger another defense, in the form of a denial. But rules about commenting don't have to be logical. Just because we can't say something about ourselves, doesn't necessarily prohibit our hearing others say it. In fact, we're probably all the more sensitive to it.

Who's Responsible for the Feedback? Looking back, there seems to be something unsatisfactory about this chapter. We'd like to tell you some sure fire ways of getting the feedback they're not sending, but there just isn't any way that works all the time.

In order to have a sure fire way of extracting unsent feedback, you'd have to know how to make other people do what you want. If you knew that, you could have just about anything you wanted. If you wanted money, you'd just apply your technique to make people give you money. If you wanted respect, you'd make them give you respect. And if you wanted feedback, you'd make them give you feedback.

Your final recourse, to get things on track when you can't figure out what they're not saying, is to comment on your own internal state:

"I'm getting the feeling that you're trying to tell me something, but I can't figure out what it is. Can you help me?"

This technique isn't guaranteed to retrieve the feedback, but it does put the responsibility back on them. After all, it's *their* message.

Experiences

1. Make a list of all the rules about commenting that you notice in yourself in one day at work.

2. Make a list of all the rules about commenting you think you see others using in one day at work.

3. If you know someone — your boss, for instance — who doesn't seem to be giving you feedback when you expect it, try writing what he says, word for word, no matter how unimportant it seems. Then try giving several alternative interpretations to his words. Perhaps check it out with him: "Is this what you meant?"

4. Sometime when you are puzzled by feedback you are receiving, ask the person, "Are you talking about *now*?" Note her reaction. If that doesn't solve your puzzlement, ask her, "Are you talking about *this situation*?" Note her reaction. If that still doesn't solve your puzzlement, ask her, "Are you talking about *me*?" Note her reaction. Note your reaction to her reaction.

5. If you go all the way through the previous experience and the other person answers "no" to all three questions, then ask *yourself*: Is she talking about *now*? Is she talking about *this situation*? Is she talking about *me*? What/who/when in the world is she talking about? Note your reactions.

Part 4

Feedback as a Process of Interaction

Assumption: *If I just work hard enough on being aware and communicate my message clearly and directly, the other person will understand my feedback.*

Fact: *Feedback is a collaborative process which one person cannot sustain alone.*

Up until now, we have looked at the internal parts of the feedback process—what happens inside the giver and the receiver. Each person is managing a complex process of perceiving, processing, and behaving, and often this is occuring simultaneously rather than sequentially.

It is appropriate, then, to think of feedback as an *interactive process,* a rapid fire and complex flow of information gathering, internal processing, and responding, often with both parties being giver and receiver at the same moment. We are often observing the reaction to our feedback as we are giving it, formulating feedback to the person while we are receiving feedback. We are likely to be comparing and integrating our past experiences with our present perceptions.

Productive feedback between people on a consistent basis could well be described as a team sport, a sport in which expert play involves several critical factors:

1. Sharing goals and needs, explicitly or implicitly, to provide the motivation of the different parties to sustain the process until they reach some reasonable degree of closure;

2. Jointly managing the climate to minimize resistance to both sending and receiving feedback;

3. Jointly addressing conflicts which emerge in the process and threaten to shut it down prematurely;

4. Allowing time for digesting and integrating feedback to prevent overload and excessive stress while being able to return later for clarification or additional exploration;

5. Managing the relationship so as to allow future interaction while maintaining a climate of directness and openness.

In this part of the book, we'll explore the conditions and skills which can help us to get on track, stay on track, and get back on track when difficulties arise in the course of the feedback process.

Chapter 11
The Context of Feedback

*A tombstone can stand
upright and lie on its face
at the same time.*

Context Lewin was clearly looking for simplicity when he came up with the formula $B = f(P,E)$ — Behavior is a function of the Person interacting with the Environment. In our terms, this is the same thing as saying the behavior of the person is determined by the context of interaction. There are many facets of context, but we have selected some of the most important elements here to illustrate the importance of approaching feedback as a team effort.

Compatible Goals The goals of the giver and the receiver do not have to be the same, but they do need to be compatible if good communication is to occur. Sometimes there is enough overlap that it is possible to sort out the difficulties. One place to look for problems is when there are two feedback messages combined into one sentence. This can happen where the goals of the two persons are different, especially when one person is sensitive to receiving an emotional message and the other person is sending with the goal of communicating a substantive message.

Bud: This report would be even more effective if it had been done on our graphic system.

Karl: Ouch!

Bud: What do you mean, ouch?

Karl: I worked really hard, and you don't like the report.

Bud: Of course I like it. I just told you it was very effective.

Karl: Oh, I thought you didn't like it.

One good way receivers of feedback can escape this trap is to ask for clarification. In this case, clarification means getting the messages one at a time. Karl was concerned about gaining Bud's approval for what he had written. The goal that Bud had in mind was to share his concern that the graphics program had not been used.

Bud: This report would be even more effective if it had been done on our graphic system.

Karl: I think I hear you saying a couple of things at once. Are you saying you're angry with me because I didn't put it through graphics?

Bud: Uh, well, I suppose I was a bit upset.

Karl: Yes, I can understand that. I was angry with myself for not coordinating the project better. And did I also hear you say you like the report anyway, even though it was done manually?

Bud: Oh, yeah. It was the best report we ever put out. You're a great writer.

In this scenario, Karl does a nice job of segregating Bud's messages. The key to his success is tackling the most emotional message first. Once that part has been acknowledged ("Yes, I can understand that. I was angry with myself."), the interaction is free of it and can proceed with the less emotional parts.

Many of us would prefer to pretend that the strong emotional part of the message doesn't exist, or at least to defer considering it. But it always hangs around, contaminating the other messages, until we face it squarely, bring it into the open, clarify it, acknowledge it, and then let it rest.

Communication Across Two Realities Well, it's easy for us to say "ask calmly and politely for clarification," but when one sends a message of great warmth only to have it received as a "cold slap," it's hard to follow that advice. It helps to allow for the fact that we are always living in a different reality than the person with whom we are talking. Thus, it may be more important to discover his reality than to have him understand our message as we intended it to be received.

Randolph: You did a fabulous job.

Juanita: You're just saying that.

Randolph: I sure was. How does it make you feel?

Juanita: Terrible.

Randolph: Why do you say that?

Juanita: Because I know how you really feel.

Randolph: How do you think you did?

Juanita: Terrible.

Randolph: Why do you say that?

Juanita: Because no one ever tells me I do a fabulous job!

Have you ever experienced a conversation like this? Think how Randolph must feel to have extended a warm hand to Juanita and have it received as a cold slap. Almost nothing is as frustrating as having your good intentions misunderstood—unless it's receiving someone else's warm hand as a cold slap. Think of how Juanita must feel!

Both Juanita and Randolph would like to communicate, but that communication is independently determined by each of them. In spite of her claim to mind reading, Juanita doesn't know how Randolph feels. In fact, she's not even sure of what he said.

Randolph, of course, knows what he said and how he feels. After this little interchange, he also knows something very important about Juanita. He can't be sure of what she said, or how she feels, but now he knows that she is not in touch with his reality. She is in touch with her own reality.

The most important step toward having a warm hand understood as a warm hand, and a cold slap as a cold slap, is simply acknowledging that there are two realities in the exchange and allowing them to be different as well as overlapping. We are so eager for a meeting of minds, a beating of two hearts as one, that we have a hard time simply accepting the two realities. Oh, how we yearn for a utopia where what you send is what I receive, whether it is a warm hand or a cold slap.

Different Priorities Sarah and Julia were identical twins. They had grown up in Manhattan and lived there all their lives. Very sophisticated city women, they had travelled to all the large cities of the world but had very little experience in the country.

They first came to Bethel, Maine two years ago for a Human Interaction Laboratory and found it a rather incredible experience, not so much for the human interaction but for the exposure to nature, because Bethel is a small country town in New England.

They returned to Bethel the following year for another workshop and had a similar experience, with the added feature that Julia met Tom and fell in love. This year they had come up again, Julia accompanied by her new husband.

They were eagerly anticipating the workshops they were taking but rather dreading the country life — not the entire country life but only the mosquitoes. In the previous two years, the twins had been badly bitten by mosquitoes. They had suffered and itched through several workshops, greatly distracting from their experiences.

When they arrived in Bethel, they met Larry, who had been in their Human Interaction Lab two years previously. As is the custom in Bethel, they greeted one another with big hugs. After hugging them both, Larry said, "Gee, ladies, you smell wonderful."

Sarah was pleased to hear that he had noticed her new perfume, and she thanked him for the compliment. "Perhaps," she thought, "what happened to Julia last summer will happen to me now." Sarah invited Larry to share dinner with her, Julia, and Tom. As they talked about their past experiences, the twins spoke of their dread of mosquitoes. Sarah said that she had almost decided not to come, simply because of the terrible memories of itching.

Larry, who grew up in the country, was astonished. "But Sarah, if you are bothered by mosquitoes, you mustn't wear perfume no matter how nice it is. Insects of all kinds, and particularly mosquitoes, are attracted by scent." To Sarah and Julia, this concept was a complete shock, an utterly new idea which they had never encountered in Manhattan or Paris or London. They really couldn't believe it, but Larry insisted.

The next day, Julia remembered to put her perfume away and actually started wearing insect repellent instead. Sarah, on the other hand, continued to wear perfume. It was a long, wet summer, but Julia went through the entire lab without a single bite. Sarah, however, got lots of bites, including one Larry gave her on her ear lobe when he asked her to marry him.

Sarah and Julia were identical twins. Larry gave the same feedback about the perfume to both. So did the mosquitoes. But Julia heeded his advice and Sarah didn't. Why?

Larry gave the twins two pieces of feedback:

1. Your perfume makes you attractive to mosquitoes.

2. Your perfume makes you attractive to me.

Both twins were naturally interested in item 1, but Julia's interest in item 2 was reduced by the presence of her husband. Sarah, at some level, was more interested in attracting a husband than in not attracting a few mosquitoes.

If the same feedback can have completely different effects on identical twins, then it's clear that:

Once again, it is ultimately up to the receiver to determine the significance of the feedback, in this case because of differing priorities.

Differing Self Perceptions — Positive and Negative

Assumption: *I, the sender, can accurately predict what you will receive as a "positive message" or a "negative message" because the value is contained in the content of the feedback.*

Fact: *The way that the receiver will evaluate feedback is determined by the life experiences, assumptions, and attitudes of the receiver, and may or may not correspond to the weighting put on the message by the sender.*

The term "feedback," as we know, was borrowed from cybernetics. In that field, the terms positive and negative feedback have quite explicit meanings. Somehow, these terms passed into the realm of personal feedback, but their meanings were left behind. Positive feedback came to be a jargon synonym for "compliment." Negative feedback became the jargon for "criticism."

Suppose you say to an audience, "you are the quietest audience I ever addressed." Some people will consider this a compliment, some a criticism, and some merely an interesting fact. How can it be called positive or negative?

A frequent determinant of our interpretation of positive and negative messages is whether it confirms or disconfirms our self perception. If we think of ourselves in a negative light, a "positive" message may be perceived quite negatively. The meaning of feedback is again determined by the receiver, so "positive" and "negative" cannot be meaningfully applied to the feedback, but only to the receiver's reaction. Remember that the next time you believe someone is criticizing you, or paying you a compliment.

Affiliative Needs – Approval, Belonging, and Nurturance

The earlier feedback interaction between Barbara and Ken captures the essence of why people don't ask for the feedback they most crave.

Barbara: Why do you look so mad?

Ken: Because you haven't told me if you like my work.

Barbara: I like your work.

Ken: Doesn't count.

Barbara: Why not?

Ken: Because I had to ask.

Ken seems to have two survival rules:

I must always have approval.

I must never ask for approval.

If his present supervisor, Barbara, isn't as articulate as he'd like, Ken becomes trapped between his two survival rules.

Ken could easily escape this trap if he approved of himself. Then his first rule would always be satisfied without having to cling to Barbara. But Ken is insecure, and craves the feedback his second rule does not allow him to ask for. Examine the interaction more carefully:

When Ken says, "Because you haven't told me if you like my work," he has very cleverly avoided asking for praise. That way he avoids a direct refusal. But when Barbara says she likes his work, he's perfectly aware that his statement really amounted to asking.

These two survival rules — I must always *have* approval, and I must never *ask for* approval — are typical of a child's view of a hierarchical power system. All existence depends on big, powerful people, and since you have no power, you cannot ask for things directly. Your only power comes from your ability to manipulate the people who have the power. You can see clearly that this is the dynamic driving Ken by comparing the "approval" interaction with the following hypothetical interaction:

Barbara: Why do you look so mad?

Ken: Because you haven't told me what time it is.

Barbara: It's four o'clock.

Ken: Doesn't count.

Barbara: Why not?

Ken: Because I had to ask.

An interaction like this seems highly implausible, because the time of day is not personal information. If Ken reacts this way over as neutral a matter as the time of day, it becomes obvious to everyone that he has a serious problem with his self-esteem. But when it's a question of approval, many of us can empathize with Ken, and that's why we pretend we're not asking for approval.

Physical Environment The feedback may be distorted by the physical environment in which it is delivered.

Irving: (angrily) You're talking too loud!

Steve: Am I causing you a problem? I thought I was talking in my regular voice.

Irving: Well, it's aggravating my headache. And someone in the next cubicle might hear you.

When you receive puzzling feedback, see what you can find out about the sender's frame of mind. What's her emotional and physical state? What is the overall situation in which you're doing this? Even when you seem to have her undivided attention, you're not the only person on her mind. In any case, few people can give crystal-clear feedback with a headache, a toothache, or itching piles.

Experiences

1. Observe people around you giving feedback and see if you can pick up different factors in the context of the situation that determine the quality and the outcome of the process. Pay particular attention to differing needs, priorities, and the nature of the physical environment. And, as always, try to pay attention to how these matters affect you when you are directly involved.

2. Experiment with your ability to be a simultaneous giver and receiver of feedback and see if you can determine the conditions under which you can do both with minimum distortion from the settings where you have the most difficulty.

3. Pay attention to the collisions in values when a person assumes that the "positive" or "negative" feedback will be received as given but the receiver reverses the value. Watch for the reaction of the giver to the "surprise" reaction and see whether it is taken as new information to be valued or as evidence that the same feedback needs to be repeated until it is "successfully" transmitted. How does the receiver react to repeated messages?

Chapter 12
Elements of Feedback Messages

*It isn't what she says but
it's the way she says it.*

We hope that you have gathered by this point in the book that one of the most important things to attend to in the feedback process is how the receiver sorts out the information. Some parts will be vividly remembered and others will not be available for recall at all. Some of what we intend may stick and some may fall by the wayside. It is important to pay attention to both, for they tell us some important things about the receiver in general or his specific state of mind.

This chapter explores four factors which can easily take priority over the substance of a feedback message. A general hierarchy can be observed, within which individuals may vary.

- *Power imposed by sender*
- *Influence desire*
- *Emotional power in message*
- *Style of sender*
- *Substance of message*

Power The use of formal power—that is, the power inherent in a position—is key to the way feedback will be received. We start out in a family hierarchy in which we may be very influential but where the power of our parents, by virtue of their position in the family, is supported by size, development, competence, and force. Virtually all of our institutions adopt this kind of hierarchy as a means of control.

Because we never completely recover from our early beliefs, people in powerful positions can make demands, be heard, exercise control, be coercive, or intimidate us. We register and remember when and how that power was exercised and whether or not it is seen as legitimate and in our interests. Where it is not seen as legitimate or in our interests, it will be a major block in our remembering and integrating the substance of the feedback.

Another aspect of power has to do with the intensity and force we use when we interact. Most of us mortals attend to two different elements of a feedback message—the wrapping and the content enclosed in that wrapping. We speak of the wrapping because most people cannot really look at the gift until the wrapping has been removed.

One component of the wrapping is the manner of delivery (Figure 12.1). Some messages arrive with a load of steam, as if launched from a catapult or blown from a dart gun. This intensity alone registers like the jab of a needle, the blow of a fist, or the slash of a switchblade. Our startled reaction or physical recoil may warn us that we've received the message, even though we haven't opened it.

Increased power is frequently shown by greater volume, sharper enunciation, or stronger admonitions about what to do with the content. You know that senders are meeting their own needs when they launch missiles with more than enough energy to simply reach you, their target. The potency of their delivery system warns you to protect your-

yourself, thus ensuring that you won't be able to receive the useful part, if any, of their message.

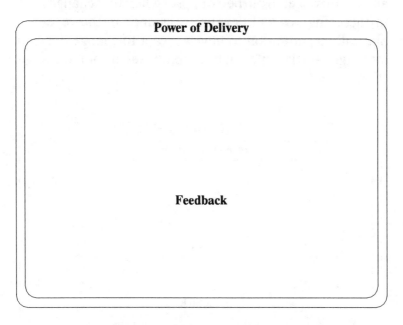

Figure 12.1The feedback may be hidden by the power the sender uses to deliver it.

If you think you really want the message, and can restrain yourself from running for the nearest fallout shelter, try to remove some of the wrapping by saying:

"I'm hearing a lot of intensity in what you said, and it makes me afraid you're trying to force me to do something. Can you say it again with somewhat less intensity?"

If all this produces is more power, then disengage yourself and head for shelter. There may be a gift inside, but it's more likely to be a bomb.

Influence Desire Influence Desire refers to the investment that the sender has for her message to be heard in a particular way and/or to generate a particular kind of response or change in the receiver. When we use feedback as a vehicle to bring about change in a particular direction, and when we get disturbed or upset when that change isn't forthcoming, we will develop resistance in the receiver. She will pay attention to how we want to change her and lose sight of the information about her in our message (Figure 12.2).

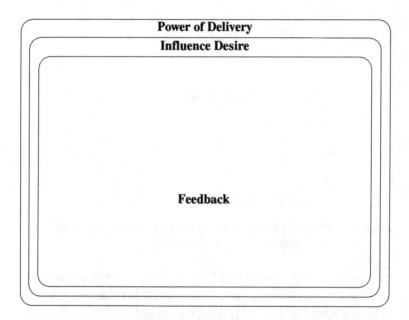

Figure 12.2 **The feedback may be hidden by the evident desire of the sender to influence the receiver.**

The more we try to control, the less influence we are likely to have. Perhaps an example will illustrate how it may be possible to say some very difficult, even outrageous, things for another person's consideration—if we communicate that they are totally free to do with our communication what they want.

Crazy Phil (by Charlie)

I was standing in one of those ticket lines at the Cleveland airport. It was 7:53, and the last plane left for New York at 8:00. All the agents were busy. Suddenly, I was jostled by a man named Phil who stepped in front of me and banged his briefcase down on my toe. He brusquely asked if I minded if he went first, since he had to catch the 8:00 flight to New York.

I was in one of those all too infrequent really mellow moods. As calmly as if I were soothing a baby, I said, "Of course not. Please go right ahead. Incidentally, I was planning to get on that flight myself."

That piece of news didn't seem to perturb Phil. Still feeling the effects of his dash from the parking lot, he panted, "I'm always late for planes. Always. I don't know why I do this. It's bad for my blood pressure. No, I don't know why I keep doing this."

I waited indulgently for a pause and then said, "You are in luck, Phil, because I do know why you do this."

Phil looked astonished. "You do? Tell me why I do this."

In the tone I generally reserve for greeting guests at funerals, I said, "You're probably emotionally disturbed."

Still panting, Phil said, "I thought it was just a bad habit."

I stood firm. "No." I picked up my bag and turned toward the gate and said as gently as I could, looking at him over my shoulder. "No, there's little chance that this kind of behavior could be explained by anything other than emotional disturbance."

I thought this would be the last word, but as fate would have it, we found ourselves seated together on the plane. We conversed all the way to touchdown at La Guardia airport.

Hearing this little feedback story, Edie and Jerry were puzzled. Why does Charlie still have all his teeth? What stopped this incident from coming to the attention of the airport police? Why did Phil actually engage Charlie with enthusiasm for the entire flight? And why, before leaving the plane, did Phil ask Charlie for the name of a therapist?

We finally concluded that Phil may have been open to considering Charlie's idea because Charlie didn't feel any investment whatsoever in what Phil did with it. Being mellow, really mellow, may just be the very condition under which one could explore almost any idea without raising anyone's hackles. Charlie has since tried this out in many circumstances, and to his own surprise and delight, still has some of his teeth.

Continued efforts to get a particular result is a clear signal that the sender intends to change us. His feedback is not an idle statement to do with as we please. It is his deliberate attempt to influence us in a particular direction. Apparently Phil felt none of this from Charlie.

By way of contrast, Charlie might have said: "Look, you jerk, I was here first. Your crappy briefcase is breaking my toes. I'm trying to get on the same flight, and I hope I get on and you don't. And, incidentally, people like you are emotionally disturbed and I ought to know because I am a psychologist." Receiving this feedback, Phil would be right to assume that Charlie has his own specific desires about what Phil should do with his message.

Emotional Wrappings Delivery power is like an outer wrapping. Once we've successfully stripped it away, the gift may still be hidden by an emotional wrapping of anger, warmth, sadness, or whatever. If the message is wrapped in anger, we might alert our system to be ready for an attack. A wrapping of warmth may open our hearts or shut off our receptors, depending on our experience with warm fuzzies in the past. A sad wrapping might trigger our immune system to minimize infection from the sender's emotion (Figure 12.3).

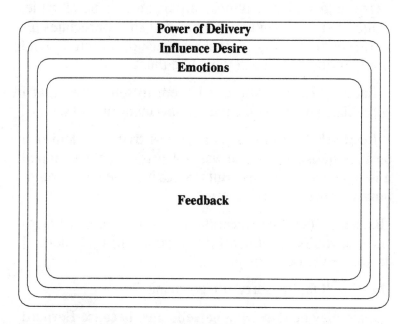

Figure 12.3 The feedback may be hidden by the emotional style of the message.

We often filter the content of a feedback message because of the emotional state we perceive in the sender. Our preferences for different emotions may differ drastically and this may influence how we interpret messages in our unique way:

Gladys: (in a loud, strident voice, fist pounding on a glass table) "Listen here, you dirty dog, how many bleeping times do I have to tell you that I think you're doing a fine job?"

Leland: (I think she believes I'm doing a good job, but, wow, is she ever angry with me. I hope she doesn't break the table.)

Long after the content has been digested, the emotional taste will linger. Leland will remember that Gladys was angry, and that she almost broke an expensive table. Quite likely, he won't remember that she appreciates his work, yet, ironically, her real feedback content to Leland would probably be something like this:

Gladys: "Leland, you don't seem to remember that I appreciate your work, no matter how many times I say so."

"Positive" Wrappings Gladys was trying to deliver a positive message, but she was so frustrated, she wrapped it in negative emotions. But it's not just "negative" emotions that distort feedback:

Bernard: (smiling sincerely, in a warm, tender voice) "Lottie, you're so wonderful that your outfit just doesn't do you or the occasion justice."

Lottie: "Oh, I'm sorry. I'll go change".

Lottie may be deceiving herself. Just because Bernard admires her doesn't mean she should abdicate her own fashion judgment. So how can you as receiver strip the emotional wrapping and access the real message? The first step is to notice your own emotional responses to her emotional wrapping. Then, comment on your responses and wait for feedback. If the other person is trying to manipulate you, her reaction will often give the game away, or at least invite clarification.

Lottie: " Gosh, Bernard. I feel warm all over when you look at me that way and say I'm wonderful."

Bernard: "Then you'll change your clothes?"

Lottie: "I'm puzzled by what exactly is wrong with my outfit."

Bernard: "You know the VP doesn't approve of low necklines or bare sleeves."

Lottie: "Oh!"

Now Lottie can make her wardrobe decisions on the basis of more accurate feedback.

Another example from the family fronts is told by Edie. Here, what starts out as a bomb ends up as a gift.

Out of the Mouths of Babes (by Edie)

I shall always remember the message I heard from my daughter, Becky, when she was six years old. I was determined to do well that evening in my image as a hostess of a small dinner party in my home. I was immersed in getting dinner pulled together. Becky was following my every footstep, holding a seemingly endless conversation, to which I had long since stopped paying attention.

In the midst of the flurry, Becky dropped her glass of milk, splattering it all over the kitchen floor. In an instant rage, I turned to Becky and barked, "Becky, I am desperate to get this dinner together and just look at the mess you've made."

Becky, who was kneeling beside the disaster, looked up at me with huge confident eyes. "Mommy," she observed, "you are angry because I spilled the milk, but you still love me. Don't you?" I forgot all about trivialities like dinner and swept her up in my arms.

A Child's Play Model for Checking Feedback This is the kind of priceless moment that lasts forever. Because Becky was absolutely clear in checking out Edie's feedback, Edie couldn't be anything but clear herself. How did Becky do it? First she directed Edie to the facts of the incident and her behavior, as she saw them. Then she announced her interpretation that their everlasting relationship was not changed. Finally, she asked Edie to confirm her interpretation, which Edie couldn't resist doing.

Becky's way of confirming feedback she thought she understood could serve as a model for adults. We may no longer spill milk, but what about when we screw up an important conference call?

1. Say what you saw and heard: "You are angry. I screwed up the conference call."

2. Announce your interpretation: "You are angry, and even though I screwed up that one call, you still think I'm an important part of this team."

3. Ask for confirmation: "Don't you?"

It seems easy enough, in theory, but even with a Ph.D. in Communication Sciences, you have to practice to get it right. Just ask Jerry.

Style Each of us has our own unique style. While we may think that it is clear and straightforward, to others it is frequently full of distractions, confusions, or new strategies which may draw our attention to the style and not the substance of our message (Figure 12.4).

For instance, our colleague Nancy Brown, gave a slightly different moral to the skunk story:

It's not what you are.

It's not what you do.

It's what they feel you might do that frightens people away.

Nancy is reminding us to use the interaction model to decipher feedback. After you have stripped away the censorship of the rules about commenting, you must start with the feelings and work backwards to the interpretation, then backwards again to the perception.

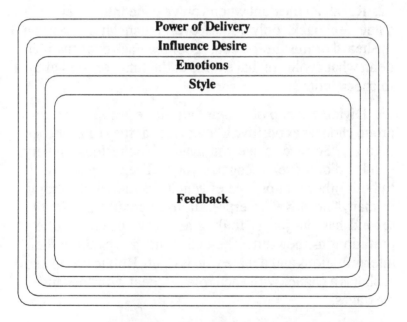

Figure 12.4 The feedback may be hidden by the style with which it is delivered.

Substance/Content At long last, we have reached the information, the substance of what a person has wanted to communicate — an idea, an opinion, a fact, or an observation. Little needs to be said about this if you can deal with the four factors that are wrapped around it. Good luck getting to the substance.

Experiences

1. In a group of people, choose as innocent a "message" as you can, something like "Jack and Jill went up the hill." Then have individuals in the group take turns delivering the same verbal message in a variety of power and emotional wrappings. For each presentation, have each person write down any messages they got in addition to the "innocent" message. Then share your interpretations.

2. Recall an incident when you've gone into a stew over some feedback, only to discover much later that you misheard or misinterpreted. Looking back over the incident, what could you have done at the time, or soon after, to check it out?

3. Divide a group of people into three groups. The first group chooses as positive a "message" as they can concoct, such as, "So nice to see you again. You're looking very good; I didn't even recognize you." Then they deliver it to both other groups, one of which has the job of finding as many "negative" interpretations as possible, while the second has the job of finding as many "positive" interpretations as they can. Then have the groups share their interpretations and debate who is right. Rotate groups, so each has a chance with each role. Repeat with "negative" messages.

Chapter 13
Additional Sources of
Difficulty

| *You kin be wrong.*

It's hard to remove the wrappings of powerful influence attempts or strong emotions. Strong desire to influence can be an important message by itself. So can strong emotions. But they are not feedback messages, though they will tend to dominate the receiver's experience. Even when these wrappings are removed, however, much of what's left may not be feedback.

In most cases, people wrap their feedback in their own experience. If you're interested in the gift of their feedback, you have to remove these wrappings, too. Once you have eliminated the censorship of commenting rules and stripped off the emotional wrappings, you move back another step in the interaction model. This brings you to the interpretations people make, adding their own experience to what they see and hear about you. (Figure 13.1)

Recording To help you unwrap these interpretations, you might want to consider a number of factors that you might be adding to the interaction:

Sonia: Obviously, you disapprove of their report.

Winona: What is it you see or hear that tells you I disapprove of their report?

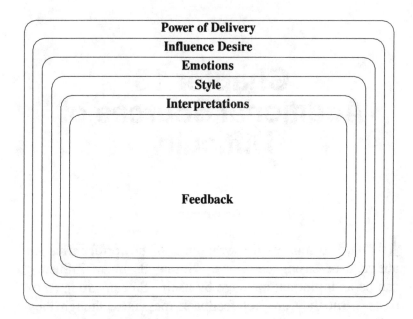

**Figure 13.1The feedback may be hidden by its wrapping of
various interpretations.**

Sonia: I can see the disapproval in your posture.

Winona: What is it you see in my posture?

Sonia: You had your arms folded across your chest.

Winona: (putting on her jacket) Thank you for telling me that, Sonia. I hadn't realized how cold I was. So let me clear that up by telling you how much I like the report. Now that I'm warm, I don't have to fold my arms when I tell you.

Winona was using a video camera as a model to guide her in unwrapping Sonia's comment. In many ways, the video camera is close to the ideal feedback mechanism, because it adds no interpretation. When decoding feedback, you can ask yourself, "Is this what a camera would see in me?

What a tape recorder would hear? What a chemical detector would smell?" Anything else is interpretation, or emotional wrapping, which you can remove by asking,

"What is it you see or hear that leads you to say...?"

Resemblance (Transference) When we see the person in front of us as if they were another person, we generate a particularly confusing form of wrapping: (Figure 13.2)

Harriet: Why don't you want to be on that committee with me? Is it something I said or did?

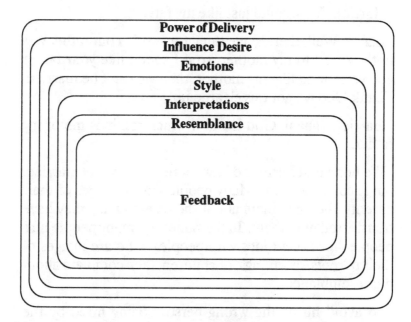

Figure 13.2 The feedback may be hidden by one person's resemblance to another person.

Larry: That's exactly the kind of question my mother used to ask when I wouldn't go shopping with her.

Harriet: What did you say to your mother?

Larry: I told her it would be just my luck to marry someone like her.

Harriet: Well, don't worry, I'd never marry you. All I want is to be on that committee with you.

Larry: Hey, why wouldn't you marry me? I'm not so bad.

Harriet: Why would I marry someone who can't stand being on the same committee with me?

Larry: Because it would be just my luck to marry someone else just like you.

Harriet: You sound just like my father!

Larry: Well, there's one thing for sure! Your father was not married to my mother, so if I sound like your father and you sound like my mother, then we can't be married. Thank God we got this cleared up!

Harriet: Thank God is right! which reminds me of my father.

We hope that Larry and Harriet really don't get married, but it could happen. Many people marry images of their parents, then complain about the resemblance they have transferred onto them. In the same way, many people hire people – or accept jobs with people – who are images of their parents, or siblings, or children, then complain about the resemblances.

To avoid hiring the wrong person, being hired by the wrong person, or making other mistakes in receiving feedback, consider the possibility that you may remind the sender of someone else. One big tipoff is the key phrase, "You're just like..." Nobody's just like anybody, even identical twins.

Why Compliments Bother Us Compliments provide a pleasant example for illustrating how the ingredients of an interaction can be used to help process feedback.

Edie to Dani: You ran two and a half miles? That's amazing!

Dani: Uh, not really. I'm not at my best now. (Dani picks up a manuscript and starts thumbing through it..)

Dani to Edie: You wrote all this? That's amazing!

Edie: Uh, Jerry did most of it.

When I'm pleased with you in some way and tell you, that's feedback. What do *you* do with compliments?

Many of us stop listening and begin to work on ways to discount what we haven't yet heard. We compare ourselves to other times we did better. We search for something to distract the complimenter. We turn the compliment around. We give the credit to someone else. Why do we do these things?

The interaction model makes our curious reception clear. Assuming we heard the compliment correctly and interpreted it correctly as a compliment, it must trigger off some survival rule. Lots of us have survival rules of this nature:

I must always be modest and never stand out.

I must never brag about myself.

If someone says something nice to you, they're trying to get something out of you.

We are embarrassed because we should not be told something that pleases us. Even though we secretly crave it, we feel guilty about it. We are ashamed, in fact, for craving praise. So we are complimented and we protest, we deny, we distort, we argue, we resist, and in no way do we accept, acknowledge, relish, reward, or appreciate the feedback compliment. To accept would be to become vulnerable, according to the rules we formed when we were about four years old.

Handling Complimentary Feedback Our reactions to compliments are fed back to the complimenter, who becomes bewildered, apologetic, apoplectic, angry, annoyed, withdrawn, and confused. Now their behavior is feedback to us that something has gone wrong with the transaction. Perhaps they didn't mean the compliment in the first place, which is what we suspected all along.

The interaction model explains why we do this to ourselves over compliments—why, for example, it's so hard for our boss or co-worker to give us praise that's really heard. It also points the way to avoiding these muddles.

When you get praise and feel yourself about to deny it, ask yourself, "How old am I now? Does praise actually represent a threat to me, here, now, with these people?" Usually, if you manage to ask these questions, you'll automatically do the right thing in response to the compliment.

But just in case you're too scared to try, how about trying a simple behavioral experiment. Next time you get praised, just say, simply, "Thank you." Nothing more. These two words indicate that the feedback has been heard and acknowledged, and there was respect for the praise and the person who sent it to us.

Try it, and notice what happens. If you don't die, try it again on the next compliment.

Implicit Comparisons Sometimes feedback seems quite specific, but contains hidden parts.

Arthur: You're a very slow typist.

Edna: Thanks. I was thinking of buying a typing drill for my Macintosh, and now I know I really need it.

Edna may be wasting her money. She might rescue her budget by remembering the old vaudeville routine:

Joe: How's your wife?

Moe: Compared to whom?

When you hear feedback that sounds important, check for comparison words, such as, slow, fast, big, small, terrific, right, wrong, or terrible. In fact, almost any adjective contains an implicit comparison. For instance,

You look stunning. (Compared to whom?)

Your work is of poor quality. (Compared to what standard?)

You're not being attentive. (Compared to whose idea of attentive?)

The answer to each of these questions is, simply, "Compared to my expectations." Even the most absolute sounding "measurements" may contain implicit comparisons with someone's personal expectations.

Arthur: You type at 50 words per minute.

Edna: Thanks. I was thinking of buying a typing drill for my Macintosh, and now I know I really need it.

If Edna has her own standard for typing speed, then Arthur's feedback is helpful. If her standard is above 50 words per minute, then she'll buy the typing drill. If it's below 50, she can save the money.

But if Edna's a little fuzzy on her own standard, or thinks she should use Arthur's standard (perhaps he's her boss), then she may make a mistake by assuming some implied standard in Arthur's feedback. He may think 50 words per minute deserves a raise, or he may think that if Edna doesn't improve, she'll be fired. Either way, it would be a good idea for Edna to check it out.

Abstracting

Pigeonhole Even when they don't react to you as a particular individual, people often pigeonhole you as part of a group of individuals. "Tall women are domineering." "American Indians are wild and brave and unpredictable." "Protestants are bigoted about Catholics." "Men with thick glasses are good lovers." (Figure 13.3)

Mark: You're really laid back.

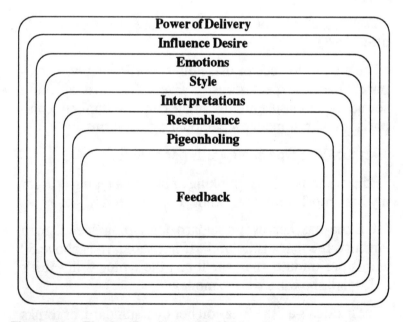

Figure 13.3 The feedback may be hidden because one person has been pigeonholed as a "type."

Jerry: I'm not sure what you mean by "laid back." What did you see or hear that gave you that impression of me?

Mark: Oh, you tall, lanky guys are always laid back. You know, like Gary Cooper.

Nobody ever called Jerry "lanky" before—or since. That's why he wanted to record the happy occasion for posterity. Like Jerry, you may be surprised to discover some of the categories they're applying to you, but if you're surprised all the time, you're not paying attention.

At 6' 3", Jerry has often been called "tall," so he's prepared for that particular pigeonhole. You can also prepare yourself to some extent for pigeonholing, though not necessarily for what that pigeonhole might imply to someone. If you want to get to the real feedback, try not to wrap it in additional emotions of your own reaction to being pigeonholed, positive or negative.

Assuming

Mindreading Ultimately, when you strip away all other sources of feedback, you may be left with that same old mysticism. (Figure 13.4)

Reva: You don't like me!

Frank: What is it you see or hear that makes you think I don't like you?

Reva: I just know.

Frank: You mean you don't see or hear anything, but you just know?

Reva: You think you're smart, but there are more ways to know than by seeing and hearing.

Frank: Do I smell like I don't like you?

Reva: No.

Frank: Can you feel my dislike in the way I touch you?

Reva: No. I can just tell what you must be thinking about me, because I didn't find that replacement part for your machine.

Our suggestion is to ignore all feedback based on mindreading. We don't doubt that some people really can read minds, but if that's so, you wouldn't want to be around them anyway.

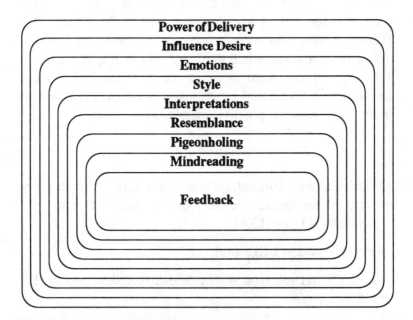

Power of Delivery
Influence Desire
Emotions
Style
Interpretations
Resemblance
Pigeonholing
Mindreading
Feedback

Figure 13.4 The feedback may be hidden because of mindreading—one person "knows" what the other is thinking.

Why Warm Relationships Stay Cold, Once They Turn Cold What are the chances that communication of a warm hand is received as a cold slap? Nobody's studied this scientifically, but, as Yogi says, you can observe a lot by just watching. And the three of us have watched a great many attempts to extend warm hands.

We've observed that most messages are intended neither as warm nor cold – they're simply messages. Our naive impressions about message temperatures probably arise from our experiences with close relationships. The closer the relationship, the greater the number of warm and cold messages, and close relationships are the ones to which we pay most attention. In close relationships, however, the number of warm and cold messages is generally not equal. Indeed, you can measure the state of a relationship by the ratio of warm to cold messages. What really makes a relationship bad is that whenever someone tries to extend a warm hand, five times out of six it's taken as a cold slap. That kind of misinterpretation happens in close relationships because to some people, "close" means "I can read your mind." And, of course, if I can read your mind, I don't have to check out even the temperature of your feedback. I know what you're saying, even if you don't say it. In fact, I know it even if you don't know it.

That's what happened when Randolph told Juanita she did a fabulous job. They have worked closely for many years, and in the early years, she was also reading his mind. Then, however, she knew that he was saying she did a fabulous job, even when he told her he wasn't pleased with her.

Nowadays, her assumption of his respect has changed, but her mind reading hasn't. And so, her perception of a cold slap in disguise led to yet one more argument. Even worse, as long as they're reading each others' minds, there's no way either of them can make the relationship better. And that's why one of the fundamental goals of consulting with teams is to teach co-workers to check out their messages.

This dynamic takes place in many working environments — very often between management and workers. A close relationship turns sour, and the same mind reading that made it close now makes it irreparably distant. We've seen organizations in which the management announced an extra vacation day to reward the employees for hard work on a project. Most of the employees, however, interpreted the day as a bribe, an attempt to set them up for lots of unpaid overtime when their project approached its deadline. In an organization like that, there's nothing a consultant can do but teach them to check out their communications.

Happily, not all of life is made up of bad relationships. In good relationships, temperature feedback isn't perfect, but it's not received at random. You may think that perfection is required, but compare it to what happens in a bad relationship. There, the reception of warm hands is worse than random. Besides, communication theory tells us that even with 51% correct reception, we can achieve as close to perfect communication as we like. All we have to do is add a checking process to the communication.

Communication theory teaches many splendid ways to add checking to a communication: shift registers, prime polynomials, Hamming codes, Huffman codes, Gray codes, and all sorts of other esoterica. But if you don't have a Ph.D. in Communication Sciences, all you need to check your communications is something even children can do — or perhaps we should say, something especially children can do.

Hearsay Sometimes feedback is not about what they've seen or heard, but what someone else reported.

Dan: You're not very reliable.

Rose: What is it you see or hear that makes you think I'm not very reliable?

Dan: Everyone says so.

Rose: Everyone?

Dan: Well, Helen said you forgot to mail a letter for her.

Rose: Oh, I didn't know she felt that way. Thanks for telling me. I'll check it out with Helen.

Courts do not allow third party reports — hearsay — into evidence. You would do well to follow their lead. Don't accept hearsay at face value, but if you're interested in the message, follow it through to its source.

Experiences

1. Is there somebody in your workplace to whom you're reacting as if they were someone who is or was important in your personal life? If so, how is this affecting your working relationship? What can you do about it?

2. Were there messages you received when you were young about people who were different from you on some dimension, such as age, sex, health, skin color, religion, amount of money, intelligence, speech style? Do these messages still affect your interpretation of their feedback in any way? Do they affect the kind of feedback messages you send, or don't send, to them? Which ones in particular are you still struggling with? Where do you think you could find the best help? What would happen if you went to one of these people and said, "I'd like to get into a clear, mutual feedback relationship with you, but I'm having trouble because of rules I learned when I was little. Would you like such a relationship? Can you help me out?"

3. What do you do with compliments?

4. This is an experience you can have with a "partner." One partner delivers a feedback statement that is as "absolute" as possible, such as, "You're great to work with!" The second partner then has to construct a comparative interpretation, such as, "And who did you work with before?" or "Even better than John?" Keep up the interchange, with the first partner trying to free the statement from all comparatives and the second trying to discover them. Then reverse roles; finally, discuss the experience.

Chapter 14
Checking Out
Interactive Feedback

| *Suspicion ain't proof.*

Getting the Most Information Once you get past the point of dying every time you get a compliment (or a complaint, for that matter), you can turn your attention to extracting information from feedback. Once you are in the here and now, your adult self knows that feedback is information, up to you to believe or not.

Sarah, being a city person, had a hard time believing that perfume really affected mosquito bites — so it was easy for her to reject information about perfume. Edie and Dani, being raised as proper young ladies in the Twentieth Century, were taught to believe that their accomplishments counted for nothing — at least when compared with men's accomplishments — so it was easy for them to reject information contained in compliments.

To believe feedback — to fit it into our current pattern of thoughts, beliefs, and values — we must overlap that feedback with what we already know. The more information there is in feedback, the less it will overlap with what we already know, so the more it will require rethinking, reorganizing, revaluing, and replacing that which we already "know."

It is also true that change creates instability, and maximum information would ultimately mean that our sense of identity would be threatened, at least temporarily.

All of this adds up to an important principle we can use in deciphering feedback:

The feedback that could give us the most information is the one that we're least likely to believe.

Consequently, whenever you hear feedback that seems unbelievable, even crazy, that's the time you ought to pay closest attention. You don't have to believe it, but you really ought to pursue it with an active and open mind. So here's another Maine story, about how Charlie does it.

Surprises (by Charlie)

Some years ago, I presented a weekend workshop with a group of sixty psychologists in Maine. Zelda, the organizer of the workshop, told me that she had really been looking forward to knowing me, so I cornered her when the workshop was over.

Charlie: Well, what have you found out about me?

Zelda: I think of you as a very private person.

Charlie: That's funny, I think of myself as a very public person.

Zelda: Oh, no!

Charlie: Well, which of us is right?

Zelda: I'm right. You may look like a public person, but it's because you know how to be private in public better that anyone I know.

Charlie: But a public person is transparent. You can see right through their skin to their insides.

Zelda: Where did you ever get that idea?

What was obvious to Zelda, and probably to everyone else, was brand new to me. I thought of myself as a strong extrovert. I felt totally transparent to all, but especially to Zelda.

The "See How It Feels" Strategy Although Charlie was flabbergasted, he didn't feel that Zelda's comment was an attack, a put-down, or a complaint. To him, it was simply a Zelda observation. Since Charlie thinks he's so transparent, let's look at what went on inside him that allowed him to be flabbergasted without becoming apoplectic:

"Although Zelda's remark was totally out of sync with my image of myself, the strength of her conviction made me hesitate to dismiss it out of hand. Moreover, my weekend experience had given me an image of Zelda as an astute observer of human beings. So my image of Zelda and my image of myself were in conflict, and something had to be done about it.

"I tried my 'see how it feels' strategy. Would thinking about myself as a private person help me organize and understand some of my past experiences better than thinking about myself as a public person? It seemed okay. Oh! As a matter of fact, thinking of myself as a private person helped me understand why I have often felt misunderstood. It felt good to understand that."

In feedback, you may hear something about yourself that surprises you because it seems to contradict your self-concept. At that moment, you have a choice. You can reject the feedback, or you can take it in and play "see how it feels." Of course, if you don't feel that the other person is trying to change you or get something from you, it's easier to play with the new idea.

How do you play "see how it feels...?." First, review the new idea in the light of puzzling experiences from the past. (If your past contains no puzzling experiences, that's the most puzzling experience of all.) Next, if it helps you make sense of those experiences, you can swallow it. If not, you can spit it out and stay with your original self-concept. You'll know if it makes sense because it will feel good to understand yourself better.

At the same time it makes you feel good, sometimes the new understanding also makes you a bit uncomfortable, like when you buy a new car. You like the car, but it doesn't feel like the old, familiar one. Maybe the knobs aren't all in the right places, or the accelerator is a bit tight.

In Charlie's case, for instance, he wasn't sure he liked this new idea of being a private person. How did he deal with it? "I realized that the difference between a public person and a private person was whether or not you disclosed yourself, not whether or not you appeared in public. So a private person can become public at any time, simply by disclosing. And vice-versa."

Satir's Medallion: A Feedback Safety Device Virginia Satir has suggested an effective way to deal with the situation in which feedback is offered in a time or place or manner that is too threatening. Imagine that you are wearing a medallion, which on one side has the message:

"Yes, thank you, I'd like to hear about that just now."

On the other side of the medallion are the words:

"No, thank you. I'm pleased that you offered, but it doesn't fit for me just now."

The medallion reminds you that you always have a choice whether to accept or reject feedback, no matter how it is offered. The medallion illustrates a paradoxical fact about feedback:

Fact: *The one skill that can do the most to increase the quantity and quality of feedback is the ability to say "no" to feedback.*

This chapter can be summarized in three words: Check It Out. In case you haven't read the previous chapters, we're not talking about supermarkets. We're elaborating on the theme of reacting to feedback, not by jumping to conclusions, but by clarifying the information.

In previous chapters, we've seen how the intentions and emotional state of the sender can be mixed in the feedback message, and how commenting rules can censor essential information. We've also seen how the receiver's emotional state can muddle the interpretation of the message. Yet even when the information is purified of these elements, there remains the possibility of complete or partial misunderstanding. That's why, even when we know what the feedback says, we have to check it out.

Charlie's Best Lecture

Judge: Charlie, this has been one of the best weeks of my life. I feel like I have been given a new lease on life. One of the events that has made the biggest impact was your lecture at the beginning of the week.

Charlie: That really makes me feel good. That kind of feedback is what makes my work so rewarding. By the way, which lecture impressed you?

Judge: I'll never forget it. It was about the difference between the Here and There and the Now and Then.

Charlie: Judge, the concept I was trying to get across was the difference between the Here and Now compared to the There and Then.

Judge: That's what I said.

Charlie: In that case you'll love the one about the Near and Dear and the Far and Rare.

Judge: That's very clever, the Near and Far and the Rear End Dear.

Charlie: Thanks again, Judge, I can't tell you what this means to me.

Checking Non-specific Feedback Lecturers, authors, politicians, and other public performers are all easy prey to flattering but non-specific feedback. Other workers are not so gullible, but they, too, get caught once in a while. If you examine Judge's statement carefully, you'll find that it's all about her. She mentions Charlie's lecture, but says essentially nothing about it that he could use as feedback.

A useful test for checking feedback for information content is to ask yourself:

What might I do differently, or continue doing, as a result of this feedback?

In Charlie's case, if he had listened only to Judge's original brief comment, there's probably just one answer to this test question: If he wants to change people's lives, he might continue giving lectures, or at least that particular lecture. He might also conclude that it was important to give that lecture "at the beginning of the week." These are certainly important conclusions, and if they satisfied Charlie, he might have been willing to stop there and not ask Judge for clarification.

But Charlie was paying attention to feedback beyond the face value of Judge's words — feedback that suggested that there might have been a difference between the message she sent and the message he received. First there was the non-specific content: Charlie had given several lectures "at the beginning of the week." Second, he had noticed previously that she seemed to be bubbling with enthusiasm, and switching rapidly from one topic to another. She seemed a bit out of control of her body movements, and her eyes were not on his as she talked to him, but flitting from one piece of furniture to another. He had seen this sort of behavior from Judge all week, and he wondered if she had really followed any of his lectures.

Charlie could have simply ignored what she said, but he truly wanted to improve his lectures, or at least not change the best parts. So he checked it out: "That really makes me feel good. That kind of feedback is what makes my work so rewarding. By the way, which lecture impressed you?" That one little question certainly got some useful information, though not exactly what Charlie had been hoping for.

How to Ask in Tough Situations Charlie's situation was a lot easier than that of, say, an employee in a review:

Boss: You're doing a fine job. Keep it up!

Akim: (Swallow; silence.)

Suppose your boss told you that. Would you feel perfectly free to check it out?

You may be reluctant to discover a difference between the message sent and the message you hoped was sent. You may be just as reluctant to discover that the message was really what you feared. When you discover that your hopes and fears are obstructing the flow of specific information, just touch your medallion to remind yourself that you don't have to swallow anything. Then go ahead and say something like this:

(a) I really appreciate your offering me that information.

(b) I usually find that the most specific information is the most useful.

(c) Can you tell me more about that?

It's as easy as a, b, c. Knowing that you don't have to ask for specific information, or any information at all, frees you from some of the emotional burden. You don't have to apologize for what you hear as criticism. You don't have to discount what you hear as praise. You don't have to promise that you'll use the information. You don't have to blame your boss for not being clear. You simply have to ask for specifics, for your own potential benefit. Once you have it, you can do with it as you please.

Experiences

1. Can you recall a time when you were pleased with something new, but also uncomfortable at the same time? Were you able to tell the difference between the two feelings?

2. Recall a situation in which you got puzzling feedback. Think of three ways you might have checked its meaning. As you think of each way, notice your emotional reaction.

Part 5

Facilitating Improved

Interactions

All three of us are professional consultants/trainers who earn our living helping people improve their interactions. As we go about our work, we encounter a surprising number of people who don't believe our work is possible. Their objections seem to fall into three categories:

Fantasy: *Feedback is not a learned skill.*

Fantasy: *Feedback is easy to learn.*

Fantasy: *Feedback is impossible to teach.*

Let's look at each of these in turn.

Feedback is not a learned skill. If this were true, there would be no sense trying to learn it, and thus a waste to hire someone to facilitate it.

Feedback is easy to learn. If this were true, then it would be a waste of money to hire someone to facilitate feedback.

Feedback is impossible to teach. If this were true, there would be no sense hiring someone.

We know these are fantasies because we see people learn, we see them struggle to learn, and we do things that help them learn.

Chapter 15
Clarity and Intimacy

*Do not feed nuts to a
man with no teeth.*

Giving feedback starts with your intention, though intentions may not be enough. You may want to persecute me, exploit me, hinder me, confuse me, victimize me, diminish me, disarm me, immobilize me, or demolish me. On the other hand, you may want to help me, inform me, encourage me, enlighten me, or improve me — but, as we've seen, you may wind up harming me even if your intentions are honorable.

One thing that gets in the way of our good intentions is our lack of skill, but if the intentions are not good in the first place, sharpening feedback skills is like sharpening a weapon.

Fact: *The first skill you must cultivate is the skill of clarifying your intentions.*

The Country Girl and the City Girl Maria, from Manhattan, New York, and Willa, from Manhattan, Kansas, were working on a Department of Energy project to improve the delivery of energy to rural areas. They were walking along a dusty gravel road near Alma, Nebraska, discussing how they were going to sell a pilot study to the town. Occasionally a car would drive by, stirring the dust in its wake, and Maria would turn her back to avoid becoming engulfed, face forward, in the dust.

After the third car passed, Willa said, "You may not know the side effects of your desire to avoid the dust. When a car goes by, local people are waving at us, and you are turning your back."

When the next two cars came by, Maria faced them, waved heartily, and then put her head down until the dust settled. Suddenly she felt more in tune with the natives, and resolved to bring some of this warmth back to the cold, bleak city.

Clarifying Your Intentions This example reminds us how feedback can empower. Willa, from the Little Apple, observed something that Maria, from the Big Apple, had neither seen nor considered. Maria was a person who highly valued human interactions, but her ignorance of country culture made her look like a high-and-mighty city slicker to the natives. When Willa shared information that touched on important pieces of Maria's value system, she still left her colleague a choice. Maria wound up feeling much more in touch with herself and her environment.

Willa intended to empower Maria, and that's a good start. When you're looking into your own intentions, you can start by asking,

Do I want to empower them — to offer them more choices than they currently have?

If the answer is "no," then hold your tongue. If the answer is "yes," then ask yourself,

Why do I care about empowering them?

The answer you're looking for, deep inside yourself, is based on a simple fact:

Fact: *Better relationships empower both parties.*

Therefore, I want to improve our relationship because the better my relationships, the more I am empowered. This is the only answer that really justifies the time, effort, and risk of offering feedback.

This answer clarifies many puzzling feedback relationships. Recall the case of the manager who was tempted to comment on the way an employee spent her evenings, because he saw her yawning and not paying attention in a meeting. If he wants to improve their working relationship, then he may decide to comment on how her yawning and not paying attention is affecting that relationship. He might talk about how distracting it is to him, and how annoyed he gets when he has to repeat something for her benefit. He is saying, in effect:

I want us to improve our working relationship, and here's some information about what's getting in my way.

But if he discovers a powerful urge inside himself to make some remark about the way she spends her evenings, then maybe what he really wants to say is something like this:

I want to improve our relationship outside of work, and so I'm commenting about what you do outside of work and how thinking about it affects me.

He may not be aware of this urge, but you can be quite sure that she'll sense it when he comments about her evening activities. And then their relationship will be off on a new path. Whether it will be up or down or around the town is anybody's guess. So before he opens his mouth, he'd better get straight in his mind what he really wants from their relationship.

Improved, Not Closer, Relationships As we've seen, the one thing feedback always does is modify the relationship between giver and receiver.

Fact: *Improving a relationship doesn't always mean making it closer.*

You might want to improve a relationship by giving the other person clear information that they should stay away from you, and that's a perfectly good reason to take the risk of telling them. To improve your relationship with a friend who's calling too often, you might offer this feedback:

"When you call me several times a week, I lose time from my work, which is more important to me than talking to you. I think that one or two calls a month would be about the right number for me."

To improve your relationship with a casual acquaintance who's been annoying you with calls, you might say:

"The last five times you've called me, I was not interested in any of the things you had to say. I would prefer that you not call me again, but that instead you would write if you feel the need to share something with me."

To get rid of an irritating salesperson, you might say:

"I'm not interested in buying a new liability policy, or discussing insurance policies, over the phone. Please do not call our office again." (Hang up.)

The Receiver is Still in Charge of What She Receives
None of these attempts may "work," because the other person has a choice about what to do with your feedback. You might think that these messages are so clear that they could not be misunderstood, but even the salesperson might call back.

Fact: *The receiver is in charge of perception, but the sender is in charge of how many times the message is sent.*

One choice, then, is to repeat your message, perhaps putting it a different way.

It's always a choice, the ways we attempt to integrate the feedback that we receive. We can choose to interpret feedback as criticizing, demanding, contradictory, complimentary, inaccurate, worthless, "right on," or demeaning. Or we can experience feedback as empowering. The salesperson could think:

Boy, there's a person with so little sales resistance that they're afraid even to talk to me. I'm going to call that one back and keep pressing.

Or your annoying friend could think,

Gosh, she sounds really busy. I'd better keep in close touch with her, and give her lots of important advice about how to avoid burnout from overwork.

Because the receiver has a choice, no method of giving feedback is going to "work" all the time, but there are ways of giving feedback so that it's more likely to be understood. There are also ways that are more likely to be misunderstood. For instance, Willa could have demanded of Maria, "Why are you such a snob?"

Closeness and Ease of Understanding In the final analysis, though, the choice of how to perceive feedback belongs to the receiver, whatever the intention of the giver.

Fact: *Of all the factors that influence the ease of understanding feedback, the most significant and confusing is the closeness of the two participants.*

When I don't know somebody at all, it is difficult for me to decipher their feedback. As I get to know them better, I begin to understand their way of communicating, and their intentions toward me, so feedback gets easier to understand. As we grow closer, I begin to *know* what you're doing, without requiring elaborate explanations.

Paradoxically, after a certain point, that very knowing becomes an impediment to my understanding your feedback. Instead of really listening to you in the here and now, I'm paying more attention to what I know about you from the past. If we're extremely close, you may find it next to impossible to convey a message to me with really new information.

Fact: *Feedback is easiest to understand when the giver and receiver are neither too distant nor too close.*

In our relationship there's a distance at which it's easiest for you to send me feedback that I'll probably receive correctly. For most of us, this is about the distance we typically have with co-workers on the job.

When I'm more distant than this, as in the case of a telephone insurance salesperson, I really don't know what kind of message will be effective. Because I don't know, I may get nervous and lose everything I know about being effective. High-pressure salespeople looking for a one-time sale count on this disquieting effect.

When I have to deliver an important message to you, and we are very close, I may get nervous from fear of changing our relationship. If I give myself these disempowering messages at the same time you assume you know what I'm saying, your feedback circuit is in serious trouble. The same thing is true if I assume you will understand me, but the closeness is causing you to generate internally disempowering messages. That's why it's so hard for a wife to teach her husband to drive, or a father to teach his teenaged daughter about the dangers of drugs. And, if relationships at work become too close, it can similarly interfere with mutual learning.

Do I Have to Work So Explicitly on My Messages? Some people react badly to the idea of consciously shaping their feedback, especially to those who are close to them.

If she really liked me, I wouldn't have to be careful about what I say, because she would understand me.

If I really liked her, I wouldn't need to think about what I'm going to say. The right thing would come instinctively out of my mouth.

These are the same old mind-reading and magic tricks. If you believe in such things, we can't do a thing for you.

Other people react badly because they think that explicit attention to their feedback is manipulative, whether of those close or those far away.

I can't use my knowledge of the closeness/understanding curve to drive this solicitor away. It's manipulative.

I can't work to be clear to my employees about their performance. I would be manipulating them with my superior understanding of how feedback works.

Well, it is manipulative, in the sense that you are attempting to help people understand your message. If you don't want them to understand your message, why are you sending it in the first place? And if you send a message, the effort required to be understood will be greater for those closest to you and furthest from you.

Fact: *The effort required to understand feedback is least when we're neither too close nor too far.*

Fact: *You have to make an effort to speak to everyone in the language they will understand.*

Making this effort to be clear isn't being uncaring. It isn't being manipulative. It's merely being clear.

Experiences

1. The following case illustrates how intricate is the connection among closeness, feedback, and empowerment:

Wally is a terrific office manager. He loves his work, and he loves the people he works with. If his performance improves while working with someone, Wally thinks they have a close relationship.

Edie came into Wally's organization to facilitate a one-day workshop on team building, trust, and closeness. At the end of the day, Wally was cleaning up in preparation to go out to dinner with the group when he noticed that there was a big hole in the seat of his pants. At dinner, he asked the group if anyone had noticed the hole. Over half the group said that they had. Wally left the dinner and didn't come back for the evening session. He said he did not want to be associated with people who thought they were in a close trusting relationship, but wouldn't give you feedback when you were walking around with your skin showing through a hole in your pants. Discuss this case from the point of view of Wally, the other participants, and Edie. What might each party have done differently. Why do you think they didn't exercise any of these choices?

2. Florence Zeigarnik was a psychologist in Germany in the 1930's. In exploring the concept of psychological tension she came across a very important psychological principle which is now called the Zeigarnik effect. The Zeigarnik effect is the tendency of people to have longer memory for uncompleted tasks than they do for completed tasks. For example, if you apply for twenty jobs, and nineteen accept you but you don't hear from the twentieth, many years later you'll be more likely to remember the one company you never heard from.

Can you recall some uncompleted transaction, when you were expecting feedback from someone and never got it? Or when you got feedback, but were never able to make sense of it? What would you have to do to put that memory to rest?

3. The power of the Zeigarnik effect is particularly important for me to remember (which will, of course, be easier if I do not understand it completely) when giving feedback that I hope will drive away someone who wants to get close to me.

When I give such feedback, such a person may very well experience his interaction with me as an incomplete task. He will therefore persist in trying to convince me to spend more time with him so that I will really get to know him.

Discuss the kind of feedback strategy that might be effective in overcoming the Zeigarnik effect when you are trying to drive someone further away.

Chapter 16
Clarity and Self Worth

| *Some folks throw too much dust.*

Parenthetical Poppycock Carla had a curious and annoying habit of asking three questions every time she wanted to ask one. Some of the people at the office, like Ralph, had a great deal of difficulty talking to her about this habit.

Carla: Are we going to use the new format? Do you think that this format will be valid for a long time? Can we stall the boss for a while, until the format changes?

Ralph: I know that this may sound weird, Carla, and it may just be the way I see it, and I hope you feel free to take it or leave it, and I am not all sure that this will be relevant, and please don't be hurt, Carla, because that is not my intention, and others may be able to say this better than I can, but you are really confusing.

Carla: Whaaaat?

What's going on here, anyway? Why would a nice guy like Ralph go to so much trouble to keep from giving a nice person like Carla a straight message? Why doesn't Ralph say, "Carla, I don't understand a word you're saying?"

Perhaps Ralph is tentative because he's got a crush on Carla. This closeness results in several internal disempowering messages:""

1. I don't want to hurt her feelings.

2. She'll reject me because my ideas are different.

3. She might get the wrong message, and then what will she think of me?

4. I don't want her to think I'm trying to influence her. It's best if she thinks it's her own idea.

5. I don't want to influence her. I want her to like me for her own reason, just the way I am.

6. Just what do I want to say to her, anyway? I mustn't make a mistake.

Unfortunately, none of these reasons has anything to do with the message as delivered, so if Carla wasn't confused before, she certainly is now. What confused her was Ralph's prolonged, parenthetical preambles, a typical example of *parenthetical poppycock.*

If you study Ralph's internal messages, you'll notice the curious fact that much parenthetical poppycock arises from his attempts to improve the quality of his feedback. The harder he tries, the more poppycock he generates. The length of the preamble is directly correlated with the tension of the sender, and can be used to diagnose that tension.

Fact: *The more you attempt to improve the quality of the feedback by increasing the quantity, the more poppycock you generate.*

Stopping, the Universal Intervention for Poppycock
Quite often, the parenthetical poppycock carries a more powerful message than the content itself. Carla could interpret Ralph's poppycock as a sign that he is nervous because he likes her. But she could just as well take it to mean he's saying, "You're such a fragile person that I have

to package what I have to say in fluff to keep from break-ing you into tiny pieces." The two interpretations could lead to quite opposite reactions on Carla's part.

What can poor Ralph do when he realizes that he's pour-ing out parenthetical poppycock? We would suggest the following options:

1. Stop and breathe.

2. Stop and say, "I'm confused. Let me start over."

3. Stop and say, "I'm confused. Can you help me out?"

4. Stop and ask himself who he is trying to protect, Carla or himself.

5. Stop and say, "I think I'm more concerned with the delivery of this message than the message itself." Then wait for Carla to comment.

6. Stop.

Notice that all six parts of Ralph's prescription begin with a "stop."

Fact: *It takes time to construct empowering feedback.*

Fact: *Nobody can consistently construct empowering feed-back when under pressure.*

That's why anyone who feels personally disempowered cannot construct empowering feedback — they always feel that they're under pressure. And that's why it's important to remember this fact:

Fact: *Stopping is always a possible facilitation.*

What You Can Accomplish When the Pressure's Off
You might find it interesting to contrast Ralph's feedback with Mona's way of dealing with the same behavior of

Carla's. Notice how Mona also gets started badly, but uses the stopping facilitation to get back on track:

Carla: Are you going to take that course, Mona? Are you hoping to get a degree? Do you think I could benefit from the course?

Mona: Uh, yes. I mean no. I mean maybe.

Carla: Will you be taking the early session or the late session? Do you think there is a difference in the instructors? I really need your help, can't you be clearer?

Mona: *(She now pauses, goes inside herself, and acknowledges that she didn't handle her first message very well. She then externalizes her feelings about Carla and about the interaction.)* Carla, I'd really like to give you information about this course, but when you ask three questions in a row, I get confused about how to answer them. I'd like you to make it easier for me by asking one at a time, and by giving me time to think about my answer.

Carla: Do you think I could?

Carla's way of asking three questions de-energized Mona. Mona wasn't too close or too distant from Carla to talk about her feelings, so she said she felt confused. This empowered Carla to realize that all three of her questions were important—one at a time. Carla couldn't get the information she wanted unless she separated the questions, and the person she questioned couldn't feel that she had communicated.

Mona could have just gotten angry, or continued stumbling in her attempt to respond to all of Carla's questions at once. Instead, she took the time to construct feedback that gave Carla both insight and something she could do about implementing that insight.

Ratchetting Ralph has a harder task than Mona because he wants to be close to Carla and feels unsure about himself. To do a better job in this interaction, he needs to construct the kind of self-feedback that will empower him. But when he feels bad about himself, he loses his power to construct empowering feedback. Instead, he feeds himself the same kind of disempowering parenthetical poppycock:

Ralph (to himself): *Oh, my God! I've been getting her all confused with this parenthetical poppycock of mine! I just know that Carla is going to misunderstand, and think I'm terrible. I'm always doing stupid things like that, and now I'm going to feel terrible for this whole day. Then I'll be depressed tomorrow because I missed such a good opportunity to get closer to Carla, and I'll be even more lonely all week, and I don't dare ask her for a date after this. I'll probably get drunk trying to forget all this, and I don't know what's going to happen to me.*

We often put ourselves into this kind of vicious circle even when no other person is present. In terms of Satir's Interaction Model, the output of one interaction sequence is fed back into our own input rather than out to another person. In cybernetics, this sort of cycle is called a "closed internal feedback loop."

In psychology, it's called "ratchetting" because it locks, like a ratchetting device, the previous cycle's output as a perception of the outside world, rather than as a meaning we have assigned by our own internal process.

A Process to Stop Ratchetting

Fact: *If you are so inclined, you can transform ratchetting into empowering feedback*

Accomplishing this change takes a deliberate effort and commitment. This is how you can do it:

1. You *experience* a strong feeling, either good or bad, that you get from thinking some thought.

2. You *acknowledge* that feeling, rather than putting any energy into denying it.

3. You quickly explore what *meaning* you have given to the thought that has made you feel that way.

4. You *accept whatever you discover as information* — interesting, informative, and potentially useful.

You may not have realized you were ratchetting You may have known very little about why you were doing it, why you continued to do it, and whether or not you wanted to do it at all. You may not have understood that you could learn about yourself by giving yourself feedback, or even that you could change your pattern if you choose to.

It would be easy for Ralph to react to all these realizations by cursing himself for his previous stupidity, but this would only lead to more ratchetting. Instead, he can simply apply the empowering feedback process to these thoughts and feelings, saying to himself,

1. *I'm feeling stupid, inept, and alone.* (**experience**)

2. *I really am feeling alone.* (**acknowledge**)

3. *I'm feeling stupid and inept because I bumbled that interaction, and alone because Carla may not like such a klutz.* (**meaning**)

4. *I can't make Carla like me anyway, though it would be nice. And, it's okay to be embarrassed and to feel stupid — everyone does at some time. In fact, it's rather amusing to discover that I'm part of the human race, and maybe Carla*

will like me for just that reason, especially if I don't try to hide my feelings from her. (accept as information)

When you give such feedback to yourself, based on awareness and acceptance of your feelings, then all this learning becomes possible, and you become empowered. In Ralph's case, he may become empowered to stop what he was doing, move out of his own ratchetting mind, and start afresh with Carla by talking about his feelings.

Preventing Ratchetting with the Feedback Response Ralph will help himself if he remembers that he doesn't have to give feedback to Carla. All he has to do is respond to her, be aware of his response, and, if possible, comment about what's going on inside of him. Since you only give feedback when you want to improve your relationship with a person, then you can apply this implicit preamble to every feedback statement:

Preamble: *I'd like to have a different relationship with you, so I want you to know that when I see you doing X, then I feel Y, and I want Z.*

Fact: *If you choke on saying these things, then you shouldn't give the feedback.*

This preamble is primarily an internal test to see if you should offer feedback at all. If you do decide to give feedback, you may not actually have to utter all of it. But don't fall into the romantic fantasy:

Fantasy: *If the situation is difficult, it's best not to be too explicit.*

This fantasy is one of the reasons you slip into ratchetting, because everything you can think of saying explicitly is censored by one of your commenting rules. Therefore, you can prevent ratchetting from happening in the first place if you remember these facts:

Fact: *The more difficult the situation, the more explicit you may have to be to resolve it.*

Fact: *Explicitness need not be the same as tactlessness.*

Here are some examples of feedback responses with varying degrees of explicitness, some of which are quite tactful, and some of which are not, as appropriate to the situation:

"You may not know the side effects of your desire to avoid the dust. When a car goes by, people are waving at us, and you are turning your back." *(Unspoken, but understood: I like you and want to work with you often. I want our clients to like you, so I want you to know about how they're reacting to you so you'll have a chance to do it differently.)*

"Carla, I'd really like to give you information about this course, but when you ask three questions in a row, I get confused about how to answer them. I'd like you to make it easier for me by asking one at a time, and then giving me time to think about my answer." *(Unspoken, but understood: I like you, and I'd like to help you.)*

"When I hear you trying to sell me insurance, I'm angry because you're wasting my time and trying to cheat me. I want you to give me your name and phone number so I can call the FBI to stop you from doing this." *(Unspoken, but understood: I don't want to buy any insurance from a telephone sales company; I don't want to hear from you again; and if I do hear from you again, I'm going to make it very troublesome for you.)*

"When an attractive stranger in the airport hands me a flower and touches me, I get sexually aroused and confused about our relationship. I want you to go away from me, or else I want to get a lot closer to you." *(Unspoken,*

*but understood: there's no way I'm going to let this relation-
ship stay as it is.)*

Experiences

1. We all have favorite feedback that we give to ourselves
over and over again. What is yours ? And why do you
think it has to be given so often?

2. How can you get the support so that you can stop the
behavior that makes it necessary for you to have to give
yourself the same feedback repeatedly? How can you get
the support so that you can accept the behavior that makes
it necessary for you to have to give yourself the same
feedback repeatedly?

3. Feedback we give ourselves usually consists of messages we got in the past from someone else. Here's a way
to make it go away. Inside your head, listen to your
repeated feedback and try to hear whose voice is saying it.
Try to feel how old you were when you heard it. Ask
yourself, is this feedback from this person relevant today?
If not, use your medallion to thank the person for helping
you in the past, then tell them that this particular help no
longer fits today's circumstances.

Chapter 17
Increasing the Amount
and Quality of Feedback

*The really great person
makes everyone else feel
great.*

Fantasy: *Feedback is not a learned skill.*

Fact: *Learning to give and receive personal feedback is like learning any other skill — it can be done badly, or done well.*

Fantasy: *Feedback is not a taught skill.*

Fact: *Teaching to give and receive personal feedback is like teaching any other skill — it can be done badly, or done well.*

The Necessary Environment for Learning You not only learn feedback skills, you also learn how to teach others feedback skills. As with other skill learning, teaching about feedback is largely a matter of creating opportunities for people to experience feedback and to practice with it.

Without special efforts, it can be hard to obtain the ideal cast and setting for experiencing feedback. Perhaps that's why experiential workshops like those that we conduct for organizations are so popular. Of course, you can't spend all your time in workshops, and some people cannot go to workshops at all. So, you need to learn to construct your own learning environments, and to construct them for others.

Mark Twain once said, "I was always careful never to let my schooling interfere with my education," and we want to be clear that by "learning environments," we don't mean schools. So what do we mean by a learning environment? Virginia Satir has offered five characteristics an environment must have if learning is to take place. According to her, the environment must be:

- *1. Non-threatening*
- *2. Illuminating*
- *3. Apparent*
- *4. Dramatic*
- *5. Humorous*

Because we're professional trainers, we use these characteristics to design workshops, but more important, because we're human beings, we use them to design our interactions with other people. Let's look at each characteristic in turn.

The Non-threatening Environment If feedback is threatening, it touches our survival rules.

Fact: *Once we are involved in a survival issue, there's little chance that feedback will be heard.* The one exception is when we are able to stay in contact after our survival rules have come into play — at least long enough so that we can learn something about our survival rules themselves. In order for this especially important learning to take place, the climate has to be particularly supportive, so that we don't invoke our rule again, or invoke some other rule.

It's a good idea to start learning how to receive feedback on topics that aren't too important to you. In a workshop with strangers, even important topics are less threatening, and most topics seem safely removed from your day to day crises. If, in this environment, you do feel threatened by some feedback, you know you are in touch with a survival rule that is inappropriately applied — and that's feedback of the highest importance.

You can carry this lesson outside the workshop. For instance, if you're a professional manager, interaction with your employees or your boss is not the safest environment in which to practice your feedback skills. If you're not a professional speaker, however, you may be able to take feedback about your presentation style more readily than you can in direct interaction with your employees.

To create a safer learning environment for your employees, you might first practice feedback skills when giving compliments, rather than when you have a complaint. Remember, however, that although some people "can't stand criticism," others "can't stand compliments." In other words,

Fact: *What is threatening for you may be safe for someone else, and vice-versa.*

Never take for granted what will be threatening and what will be non-threatening. Check it out.

Use Your Medallion New insights from feedback never take away your freedom to be yourself. They merely give you new options to add to the old familiar ones. So, if you feel that accepting feedback information will force you to be someone else, just take out your medallion and say, as politely as you can,

"Thank you for offering me that information, but it doesn't fit for me just now."

That's all there is to it.

In cybernetics, the terms *input* and *output* are used to describe the processes of receiving and sending feedback. A more accurate word for receiving would be *intake*, not input. The word input implies that the receiver is a passive target of feedback missiles, which is not a very safe position. The word intake implies that the *receiver is in control,* and the medallion is a concrete representation of that control. That's why teaching people how to use their medallion can be the most powerful first step in creating a safe learning environment. Even without a medallion, receivers often indicate just what is acceptable and what falls out of bounds. Senders tend to be sensitive to receivers' tolerance and thus allow their messages to become controlled through self-censorship. As one consultant told us about a client, "He seemed uncomfortable when I mentioned his interaction with his boss, so I'll steer carefully in those waters." But if the consultant had taught his client to use a medallion, he would have created a less-threatening environment for his own practice in offering feedback.

Fact: *When you have a medallion, we're both less threatened.*

The Conditions for Illumination You want an atmosphere in which you have time and opportunity to discard lots of feedback. With all the potential sources of error that exist in the process of distinguishing the relevant from the useless, it's better to overdiscard than overaccept. If a discarded item proves valid, feedback about it will occur repeatedly, so you won't miss it if you look for patterns.

In cybernetics, using repeated patterns is called "separating the signal from the noise." In psychology, we call it "illumination." Watching for patterns is not the only way to extract whatever illumination that feedback may contain. In a workshop, you have many other participants, as well as experienced facilitators, to help you with this process. Most of the illumination, however, comes in moments when you are alone, outside the formal workshop setting.

Good workshops are designed to provide repeated experiences from which you can extract patterns, other people to help illuminate the meaning of those patterns, and sufficient alone time to illuminate yourself. You can design this sort of environment into your work life as well. If you are fond of saying, "I never have two minutes to myself," you may think you're looking busy to the boss.

Fact: *If you never have two minutes to yourself, you'll never extract illumination from feedback.*

Like rats in a psychology department, people often learn from being shocked. If you can't close your office door and be undisturbed for five minutes when you've just been shocked, find a place where you can hide. Otherwise, you'll just keep getting shocks without the learning.

Making Lessons Apparent by Making Them Concrete
Lectures are another environment for learning. Many lectures are non-threatening and illuminating, but though we often go away from lectures feeling illuminated, we seldom seem able to apply these illuminations to our work.

Fact: *Many people have difficulty applying abstractions to their own concrete situations.*

Experiential workshops may contain "lectures," but ideally they use material from the "here and now." That is, they deal only with things that are happening *in this room, with these people, at this time,* which is about as concrete as you can get. Outside of workshops, you can benefit most from seeking feedback that is also in the here and now, and by making less use of feedback about other times, other people, in other places. When you receive such displaced feedback, you can request that it be made more concrete, to increase your chance of learning from it.

When you are giving feedback, you may have to strike a compromise between illumination and concreteness. To be illuminating, you don't want to base feedback on one isolated example, but rather on a repeated pattern. To be concrete, however, you don't want to give ancient history examples that have been collecting dust in your drawer. We've seen how personnel appraisal systems are sometimes used in this way, as the manager builds up courage by "collecting stamps" on the employee, all of which are cashed in for the premium on appraisal day. This is not an ideal environment for learning.

Making Feedback Dramatic Increasing the intensity of your message is one way of heightening your impact.

Fact: *Because we are always struggling to preserve our models, feedback presented in a dramatic fashion has the best chance of catching our attention.*

Many experiential workshops create drama through contrived exercises that are hard to ignore. Unfortunately, most of the dramatic situations in our day-to-day work are accompanied by feelings of danger, not safety. With a little imagination, however, we can create drama without the threat.

For instance, workshop exercises often create drama through the use of modes of perception that we ordinarily ignore in the flood of words. Examples include drawings, posture, movement, touching, and simple props, such as hats, ropes, or toys. By paying attention to more than the verbal part of feedback, we can increase the dramatic impact, and through it, the learning. One of our clients starts every meeting by passing out "listening hats" that people remove to signal that their attention has wandered. When all the hats are off, the speaker gets a dramatic non-verbal message that would be difficult to duplicate in words.

On the receiving end, when you are puzzled by verbal feedback, you can solicit the same message in other forms. "Could you draw me a picture of what you mean?" "Could you show me with your body how you feel?"   Anything that gets you out of the verbal realm will increase the dramatic impact.

Keeping It Humorous Over the years, the number of "listening hats" has grown as people have donated bizarre chapeaus to the collection. A playful atmosphere helps give the message that mistakes are acceptable.

Fact: *If mistakes are not acceptable, learning is not possible.*

Watch children learning to use feedback while playing. They seem more natural than adults, less hampered by etiquette, less afraid of vulnerability, and less hesitant to change. Lots of important changes in working relationships take place on the company softball team — if the boss doesn't take winning the trophy too seriously. Is the work in your office so grim that "playing" is not allowed? If so, you'll not see much learning.

Humor works to facilitate learning in many ways:

Fact: *Humor allows us to explore alternatives.*

Fact: *Humor exposes our assumptions — that's why the punch line is funny.*

Fact: *Humor allows us to introduce new material in a safe way because you can always say, "I was only joking."*

And, of course, humor is completely portable. It can be carried into any real-life situation. Perhaps the guiding motto for setting the atmosphere for effective feedback at work should be:

Our work is too important to be taken seriously.

Experiences

1. Design some settings that would be safe enough for you to experience Virginia Satir's five major ingredients for learning from feedback. Which settings were easy for you to design? Which ones were difficult for you? Which ones do you think are impossible?

2. In what ways can you continue to get some insight and support to help you work on designing the settings that have been difficult or impossible up until now? Who can you ask for assistance? If you can't design your own setting, what new places can you go to find such settings?

3. Write down a specific problematic situation in which you were trying to get feedback—some situation that came to your mind as you read this chapter. Make note of who was involved, what was your role, and what were you trying to accomplish, then answer the following questions:

a. If you could do it all over, how would you go about asking for it?

b. Did you accept too much of the feedback you got, without deciding what to take and what to reject? How could you have helped yourself stop doing that, if it occurred in that specific situation?

4. Note the three people who frustrate you most when you try to get feedback from them.

a. Why is it frustrating?

b. In what ways have you asked that haven't worked?

c. Can you identify anything that you swallowed at the time that you now reject?

d. Replay the conversation out in your mind until it works for you—keeping aware of when some survival rules pop into your head.

5. Develop a symbol for yourself that you can use like Satir's medallion. It can be a concrete item that you can hold, wear, or show to people.

a. Try taking the time to visualize something so unique that you would not want to use it for any other purpose. Jot down the main features, such as size, shape, color, texture, weight. Put your own words on each side of it.

b. Now see who comes to mind if you were to show each side to three specific people. Show it to them until you are sure they understand the message.

c. What did you feel yourself?

d. And how do you imagine that they are reacting to the message you showed them?

e. Would you like to inscribe a secret code on the medallion that only you know is there? What would it say?

Having chosen your medallion, see if it helps you notice situations in which you have the choice of yes or no.

Chapter 18
Timing Your Feedback

> *Some folks have the*
> *hateful taint of being too*
> *soon with everybody.*

We've seen that for feedback to be effective, it must be non-threatening, illuminating, concrete, dramatic, and humorous. Each of these attributes affects and is affected by the timing with which we give feedback, as the following stories will illustrate.

Lisa's Little List Lisa was manager of software development at a medium-to-large insurance company. Ronald, who worked for Lisa, was a senior systems programmer. After Ronald had worked for Lisa for 4 years and 4 months, Lisa called Ronald into her office and told him that she was terminating his employment. When he asked why, she presented 280 pages of single-spaced grievances against Ronald that she had been keeping secretly for 4 years and 4 months.

By carefully recording her feedback for 4 years and 4 months, Lisa certainly assured that it was non-threatening, illuminating, concrete, dramatic, and rather pathetically humorous. On the other hand, she also ensured that it was not effective at improving Ronald's performance. By the time he got it, it was an iron-clad case for firing him.

This extreme story shows what can happen when feedback comes too late. Generally, the effectiveness of feedback diminishes the longer you delay in giving it. If you wait too long, you may be better off not giving the feedback at all—but only if you can truly forget about it. If the feeling you wish to communicate is still in you, then it's never too late to give the feedback—about your feeling.

You also have to balance late feedback against the potential costs of giving it too early, or at a time when the person is occupied with something else. The following story illustrates how effective feedback can be if given at precisely the right moment.

Bill's Big Bill Bill had just graduated from high school and gotten his first real job, as stockboy in Withington's Department Store. As stockboy, he had free run of the store, moving from one department to another as the need arose. His favorite department, though, was Personal Electronics. He'd always wanted one of those tiny portable AM-FM radio tape players, with headphones, but he'd never been able to afford one. Whenever he had a break in his activities, he'd wander over to the Personal Electronics department and contemplate the merchandise.

As Bill stood in the store, staring at the portable AM-FM radio tape player, he reflected how the store had so many of them, and he, who really wanted one, had none. In fact, he thought, the store had so many, it would probably never miss just one, especially with their slipshod stock record system. *It sure would be neat to own one,* he mused, hefting it in his hand. *It's so light, I wonder if I'd even feel it when I was carrying it in my pocket.*

Bill was startled out of his reverie when Sara appeared beside him and said, smiling as she would to any good customer, "Were you going to pay cash for that recorder, Bill, or put it on your employee's account?"

Bill blinked, gulped, and said, "I was thinking of putting it on my employee's account, ma'am, but first I was going to ask you about the procedure."

Bill, who never actually did anything except think about doing something, remembers this feedback today, 15 years later. And even more amazing, he still gives himself Sara's feedback whenever he is tempted to take somebody else's property. Any way you look at it, Sara's feedback was certainly effective.

Part of that effectiveness can be attributed to Sara's care to make the feedback non-threatening, illuminating, concrete, dramatic, and humorous. Most of her care was exercised in her timing. If she'd said something about shoplifting when he entered her department, it wouldn't have been very concrete or dramatic. If she waited until he had the recorder in his pocket, it would have been concrete and dramatic all right, but also very threatening and not very funny.

Feedback Interruptus Feedback that is given after something happens may already be too late. In that case, the most effective use of feedback is to interrupt a process.

Perhaps half of all feedback occurs during the period that the Bills of the world are contemplating doing whatever they are doing. Amazing? Not to Sara. As manager of Personal Electronics, she'd spent plenty of time watching Bill, and other young folks. She's noticed that he keeps doing the same thing over and over, and she's seen the fondness in his eye as he contemplates the shelf full of recorders. She has advanced to predicting how he will end something he begins.

Feedback when you think I'm thinking about doing something is just one example of feedback that interrupts my potential action. Here are some other possibilities:

When I let you know I'm thinking about doing something:

Me: I wonder what would happen if I poured glue in Mac's keyboard next time he shouts at me?

You: I suspect you'd get fired.

When I say I'm going to do something:

Me: I'm going to leave half an hour early today.

You: Then I guess you'll miss the President's special meeting.

Me: Holy cow! I completely forgot about that!

When I want to do something:

Me: I'd like to take this report home.

You: I took a confidential report home once.

Me: Really? What happened?

You: I had to spend four hours with the Chief of Security. Then I had to take a special three-day class. Was it boring!

When I start to do something:

You: Is this the first time you've been up in a cherry picker?

Me: As a matter of fact, it is.

You: I find that attaching my safety strap to the bracket makes me feel more secure when I'm 75 feet up. It's also company regulations.

When I am already doing something:

You: Opening the case that way, you've broken the seal on three of the jars of elk's liver pate.

Me: So?

You: The jars cost about $17 wholesale, and we can't legally sell them if the seal is broken. Would you like me to help you open the other 11 cases?

When I am almost finished doing something:

You: If you touch the Reset key right now, you'll wipe out your entire file.

Whichever moment you choose, you'll never know what would have happened if you'd chosen another moment — or if you'd refrained altogether. Do the possible rewards of preventing something outweigh the advantages of learning from feedback about something that actually has happened? How many jars of of elk's liver pate have to be ruined before the cost of the lesson will make it stick? Can someone really learn about wiping out files just from theory, or do they have to experience that awful feeling for themselves?

Feedback interruptus certainly puts the onus on you, the sender, for you will never know how things would have worked out really, without your help.

One Word Feedback You know that one picture can be worth a thousand words, but do you realize that, with the right timing, one word may be worth a thousand pictures? There are many instances in which a single word can act as a catalyst for intense internal feedback experiences. The words themselves are usually simple words: Oh? Well? Because? Sure? No? So? Huh? On a sunny day, you may not even need one word. Sometimes a nod, a cough, or a raised eyebrow will do the trick.

Milo: He borrowed my manual, so I poured glue in his keyboard.

Wendy: *So?*

Milo: Oh! You mean I could have done something else?

How can such a tiny morsel of feedback be so effective? Your repeating a key word just after I've finished talking invites me to do an instant replay in my own mind of what I've just said. This simple act allows me to reflect on my utterance as an outside observer.

In other words, let me play your role and I may hear it less defensively than if it came from you. I may understand that I have an internal conflict that needs to be resolved — rather than mistaking it for a conflict between you and me.

More importantly, I may find that I have all of the information I need to gain a new understanding of myself. What I was lacking was support to take the time to reflect on what I was thinking and saying about myself. Your minimal feedback, delivered in a gentle tone, gives me that time and just the right amount of support. If you were harsher, or used too many words, I would be forced to come out of my own mind, rather than stay inside it, where the work needs to be done.

Automatic Pilot A curious event happened when we were writing this chapter. As it was already past one o'clock, Charlie suggested a break for lunch. Jerry gets a little obsessive when he's writing, and he took the break reluctantly. As a result, Jerry was still mentally in the midst of the chapter while driving downtown — so he ran the stop sign.

As Jerry approached the intersection on "automatic pilot," without any indication of braking, Charlie noticed a police car parked across the street. "Isn't it a curious fact," he said in a contemplative tone, "how frequently there is a police car lurking in just the right place at just the wrong time?" This was certainly a profound observation, but so long and obtuse that by the time Jerry figured it out, he was in the middle of Elk Avenue with the police in hot pursuit. Jerry believes that if Charlie had simply said, "STOP!," he might not have gotten a ticket.

Your one word, offered at the pregnant moment, with the right inflection can serve me as a mental stop sign. It can help me check my location, the route that I've just taken, and possibly allow me to change course from the direction I was taking while on "automatic pilot."

Feedback as an Interruption There are times when a back-seat-driver yells at the driver in such a disturbing way that the driver loses control of the car and crashes. Feedback is always an interruption, but that kind of interruption is counter-productive. Charlie wanted Jerry to stop the car, not to stop driving the car.

To some extent, we're always on "automatic pilot." That's what enables us to talk and drive at the same time — or talk and think. So whenever you take your turn at talking, it's going to interrupt that part of me that's trying to think. If you want me to keep on thinking, but just change direction a wee bit, then you have to shape your feedback into the least intrusive form.

Shaping just the right feedback takes a lot of energy. Often, your energy comes out in the form of too many words, words that break too powerfully into my stream of thought. With so many words, there's also the danger that I will pick up multiple messages, which forces me to choose among them. And choosing is an act of thought, one more step removed from my automatic piloting.

Your feedback to me always carries the danger that I will perceive your intentions and motivations at the same time and distort the feedback. Your one word feedback cuts out the fat, and keeps the focus clearly on me.

There is a certain elegance about one word feedback. It allows the you to observe how I am processing my own experience. You have both verbal and non-verbal clues to help you understand where I am at each moment. And don't forget how satisfied I'll feel when I figure out something for myself instead of being dependent on you for all the information.

One word feedback is process feedback, as opposed to content feedback. Content feedback is packed with information from you to me, while process feedback simply invites me to notice my automatic pilot. Ultimately, the most powerful effect of any feedback is to create a reflection — a reflection that allows me to use my own capacity to look at myself in a mirror. The power of one word feedback is demonstrated by the success of non-directive counselling pioneered by Carl Rogers.

Countering Feedback From the Past One word feedback illustrates that properly timed feedback does not have to be full of power to be powerful. In Bill's case, Sara's few words of feedback are still working after 15 years.

What's unusual about Bill's case is that he still remembers the incident explicitly. Much of our early preventive feedback is stored in our survival rules, but usually those rules are universalized, and we can't even recall their origin. And because we can't recall their origin, we feel powerless to change them.

Because Bill remembers when he learned about not stealing, he has a choice about overriding that rule. For instance, he might be able to steal a loaf of bread to keep his family from starving, something he couldn't do if the rule were more universal, like

I must never steal.

I must never make anyone angry.

I must always finish what I start.

I must always be perfect.

In spite of their universal tone and mysterious origin, survival rules are neither more nor less than feedback from the past (then and there) which you have stored up and which are played back in the present (here and now) to compete with present information. With survival rules, the timing may be off by fifty years or more. They may be even less appropriate than Lisa's Little List, but unlike her list, they can be extremely effective at altering behavior.

Some of our survival rules contain great wisdom, but wisdom is not merely know-how. It's also know-when. Our survival rules from there and then are often entirely inappropriate for the here and now. When you hear some internal feedback from the past, like "I must always finish what I start," bring the timing up to date. Give yourself some feedback in the present, such as:

I can sometimes finish what I start, but I can also leave something unfinished when I don't like the task, when it's not really important, or I simply want to leave it.

Experiences

1. Lisa's work with Ronald, in current organization jargon, was a fine job of "documenting." "Documenting" is not a form of feedback, but a way of making a case on someone you're afraid to fire, because of Equal Employment Opportunity, Personnel Policies, or Grievance

Procedures. Documenting without feedback carried on in parallel is a mockery of the laws, policies, and procedures designed to give each person a fair shake. In some instances, the mockery has gone so far that managers are given awards for outstanding jobs of "documenting" their employees. In these systems, Lisa would have been a real winner.

Give two examples of documenting from your experience — one with feedback in parallel and one without. What are the differences between these two approaches to handling problem employees? What were the different outcomes in the two situations? Which of these situations comes closest to your organization's actual practice of "performance appraisal?"

2. *Feedback interruptus* may seem a contradiction to the rule about not giving uninvited feedback. Can you think of how the two might be consistent? Or, if they are inconsistent, how will you decide which guide to follow?

Chapter 19
Congruent Response

*You don't need help
fallin' down but a hand
up is sure welcome.*

Concentrate on Congruence We've now reached the point where one message should be clear. Don't concentrate on giving feedback; concentrate on being congruent — responding to the other person, to yourself, and to the here-and-now situation. Don't go around hunting for opportunities to give feedback, because feedback is effective only when the need arises naturally out of congruent interactions. We've also made clear that you cannot help giving feedback, because not giving feedback is also a form of feedback. It seems we have you in a paradox, but you can resolve it by concentrating on congruent interaction, rather than on "giving feedback." Congruent interaction includes giving feedback, but is not dominated by it.

Giving feedback starts you in a one-up position, and manufactures a win/lose situation. Congruent interaction is a way to move the situation outside the winning and losing dimension. In this chapter, we'll present a model or metaphor for achieving congruent interaction so as to substitute "mutual learning" for "win/lose." After all, learning is what feedback is all about.

A Way to Start Clearing Interactions The interaction model helps to explain one of the great paradoxes of human interaction:

Fact: *People respond better to you if you devote attention to their problems, but one way of devoting attention to their problems is by being candid about your problems.*

As the interaction model makes clear, many of their problems arise from trying to deal with you – to understand why in the world you're doing the "crazy" things you're doing. They have no access to your inner sequence except through your own candor, so congruent statements about you become helpful to them. Each of your authors encounters this problem repeatedly in our workshops when participants pose problems that stump us. If I'm feeling stupid, but try to hide the fact by making them feel stupid, I'm not giving them the gift of clear, reliable information. But suppose I simply say, with good humor,

"Gee, I'm having a hard time figuring that one out, and I'm feeling somewhat embarrassed to look dumb in front of the class."

This is a reasonably clear, straight comment about our inner sequence. Using this information, the participants now have a better idea where I stand. They also have a model of how they can behave as leaders when they are stumped. This opens many new possibilities for them, both as leaders and as followers – a gift which they can reciprocate by giving me accurate information about their own internal sequences – or about our external manifestations. It also opens something of a "who goes first" paradox:

Fact: *The only place you can get the gift of accurate internal information is from the other person.*

Fact: *If you don't have accurate internal information about the other person, you probably won't get it from them unless you give some first about yourself.*

The Technique of Giving Internal Information This gift-giving technique can almost be reduced to a sequence which follows the stages of the interaction model:

- *First, tell them what you perceive.*
- *Second, tell them what meaning you give to that perception.*
- *Third, tell them how you feel about what you perceive.*
- *Fourth, if possible, tell them how you feel about that feeling.*

Here are some examples:

1. "Because I see them whispering to each other, it looks to me as if John and Sarah are not participating in this discussion, even though I'm trying every technique I know to get them involved. This feeling of failure makes me afraid that you'll see me as an inadequate meeting facilitator."

2. "The way I interpret your last question seems to me that you're asking me to give you confidential information. I feel angry with you because it seems to discount my personal moral feelings, yet I feel that I have no right to be angry with you."

3. " When I find myself asking you three times when you will finish this late assignment, I feel ashamed about acting like a dictator and not trusting you, yet I don't know how else to deal with my anxiety over the project schedule."

These are difficult things to say to other people. When I apply this sequence, I am saying, in effect,

"I am vulnerable, but I am confident enough in myself and in you to expose my vulnerability."

For practice, let's try to apply this recipe to several common feedback situations.

Clarifying Observations and Interpretations Because you cannot see yourself from the outside, the most valuable information I can give you is often an observation — what I see you doing, the expression I see on your face, what I hear you saying, or how tightly my hand feels squeezed by your hand.

Some people would call these observations "facts" about how you have behaved, looked, sounded, or felt. However, I should never forget that they are not facts about you, but facts about my observations of you. That's why it helps to preface these observations with remarks that remind both of us that they are my observations.

I notice that the hem of your skirt is unravelling in back.

I heard you say that you were going to the movie, then *I heard you say* you weren't going to the movie.

Fact: *It's very easy to confuse interpretations with observations.*

Observations can only be about things you can sense. Interpretations are things you may or may not sense. Any "observation" about the other person's internal information must be an interpretation until you've checked it out. For example,

I notice that you are angry. (interpretation)

I notice that you are shaking your fist and talking louder than you were a minute ago. (observation)

When I see you shaking your fist and hear you raising your voice, I think you are angry. Are you? (combination of observation, interpretation, and checking it out)

Attempting to Influence Congruently

Fantasy: *There is such a thing as "innocent" feedback.*

Although I may believe that my observations are the most innocent form of feedback, they are contaminated by the fact that I chose to offer them to you.

I see your hands are shaking. (And I chose to mention it to you, rather than say nothing.)

Fact: *The fact that you offered feedback at all is always significant.*

My choice to tell you about your hands must have some purpose behind it, although neither you nor I may be conscious of that purpose. Otherwise, I would simply not have commented about your hands, just as I have not been commenting about the color of your shoelaces, the wart on your nose, the thread on your jacket, the rate your eyes are blinking, the fact that you are pronouncing my name correctly, the depth of your breathing, and other things I might have commented on besides your hands shaking.

My purpose might be to influence you in some way, or perhaps to influence myself. I might want you to acknowledge that you are nervous, or I might want to reassure myself that you are just as nervous as I am.

Fact: *The fact that you offered feedback at all is often the only significant part of the feedback.*

Influence attempts take many forms besides just offering observations. I may give you suggestions, advice, signals, directions, help, or manipulations to get you to take a particular next step or to understand something in a particular way.

I see your hands are shaking. If you put your thumb in your mouth, your hand will stop shaking.

I may even influence you by giving you information to help you feel okay about what you're doing.

I see your hands are shaking. Shaking is quite normal when you've just been chewed out by your client, and nothing to worry about.

Offering Reactions Congruently If I am trying to influence you, I may offer you my perceptions of how you are progressing toward goals, either yours or mine.

You're up to where you can almost get letters out on time.

This kind of feedback can also be a way to sneak in goals that I want you to have.

If you sell two more condos, you'll have enough money to redecorate our offices.

You would have a better chance of receiving the kind of information hidden in the previous examples if I gave it more congruently:

I'm pleased when I see how your typing speed has increased, because you're making progress toward your goal of being a better secretary. Besides, if you get a little faster, I won't have to type any of my own letters.

I'd really like to get our offices looking better. I'm pleased that you're selling so many condos, because the more money you have, the more choices we have about how we run our business.

The more I talk about my reactions to what you've done — my feelings, thoughts, and behaviors — the better you get to know me. But if I am a bit uncertain about our relationship, I might not want to give such information directly. It may give you power over me if I tell you how I've changed as a result of our interaction.

If that doesn't feel safe, I may be tempted to offer my reactions in an indirect way.

Fantasy: *Indirect reactions are the best way to offer* "negative" reactions.

Fact: *Indirect reactions hardly ever work, and often* backfire.

You may have no awareness that you affect anyone, so you will miss all indirect feedback about your impact. And if my indirect feedback about impact doesn't work, I may start suppressing all feedback and wonder why other people don't change their behavior. If I don't tell them, I shouldn't be surprised if they don't know.

Exposing Assumptions, Judgments, and Conclusions As a result of our experiences together, I am constantly making assumptions about your intentions, motivations, goals, feelings, past history, or current concerns. To maintain a congruent interaction, I may want to keep you up to date on what I am assuming about you, and check it out. It may be painful or awkward, but let's give it a try.

When I hear you tell me not to go to the debriefing, I assume you're trying to protect me. Is that right?

I may also want to give you my judgments — evaluations of the quality, esthetics, effectiveness, efficiency, or worth of your efforts. Again, it helps to make clear that they are my judgments, rather than absolute statements. I might want to keep from saying, "That's not a very grown up response" (my judgment disguised as a fact about you).

I might want to try,

When I hear you calling me pushy, and I cannot see how I am pushing you, I think that you may be reacting out of some earlier experience of being pushed around. Does that fit for you?

This gives you access to what's going on inside of me, so that your response is more likely to be in a useful direction.

Another thing going on inside of me is decisions I've made about what to do with my reactions to you. It's also helpful not to leave you guessing about such decisions.

When I hear your tone of voice, I conclude that you're angry with me. You may not actually be angry, but I get so upset that I cannot keep up my end of the interaction. That's why I'm leaving now. If you're willing, I'll take up this subject with you at another time. (I've decided to leave for my own protection, but I'm not leaving forever.)

Behaving Congruently I do many things in response to you besides talking. Because they are not so much in my control, you may believe my non-verbal actions over my words, when the two are not congruent.

Fantasy: *You can control all your non-verbal actions.*

Rather than try to control my gestures, physical movements, expressions, and appearance, I ought to try to notice them and see if they are congruent with my words. If they are not, what is it that my words are not saying?

What to Do when You Lack the Courage to Be Congruent When you show me your vulnerability, you open a channel that might get you information you need about yourself. The risk is that I might use this channel to attack you. It's not a great risk—but it definitely feels enormous the first few times you try it.

Fact: *It's not true risk that triggers survival rules, but the perceived risk.*

It helps to remember that you're not really exposing yourself by revealing yourself, because you're already exposed.

Fantasy: *You can hide your true feelings if you want to.*

Fact: *The more you try to hide your feelings, the more easily other people can see your foolishness. No, you don't fool anyone but yourself, but you probably don't want to believe that. In that case, you might want to face your fear by saying, out loud,*

"I don't think I've been very clear about how I see this situation, but I have a new feedback technique I want to try. Is that all right with you?"

If the response is "yes," you continue,

"This technique requires that I tell you how I really feel. Since I don't have much experience with this approach, it's rather frightening to risk telling you how I really feel, in case you should misunderstand or try to use it against me. But I do feel good about having the courage to say this much anyway."

Experiences

1. Recall something you were taught that moved you a step further away from your true self. Recall something you were taught that moved you a step back closer to your true self. Which gives you fonder memories? Which was of greater value?

2. When we give examples of precisely how to give congruent feedback in difficult situations, they may sound a bit stilted, as when we said,

"I'm pleased when I see how your typing speed has increased, because you're making progress toward your goal of being a better secretary. Besides, if you get a little faster, I won't have to type any of my own letters."

Doesn't that sound a little awkward—like we took one too many courses in how to give feedback? Of course it does, because we are taking pains to identify each component of the interaction explicitly. In real interactions, as people know each other better and better, certain components can be dropped out, or shortened, without losing effectiveness. If things get tangled, we can revert to the more complete, albeit stilted, form.

Take the feedback above and revise it into three shorter versions, for three increasingly intimate relationships.

Part 6

Epilogue

Feedback Artistry

A good friend is a man who rolls his own hoop.

We've come to the end of a long journey together, one in which we've tried to offer you what we know about feedback in human interactions. In the end, though, you are the most important component of your feedback, far more important than any lists of ideas we can provide. Whatever else you do, you will be putting your true self into your feedback, and it will show. Therefore, the only way you can become a feedback artist is to master the art of "rolling your own hoop."

All we can offer you on that score is what we've learned about ourselves, in the form of two summaries.

The Art of Giving Feedback

1. I must *take care of myself,* because if I'm off center, my feedback will be contaminated.

2. I must *feel in control of me in the situation,* because otherwise my feedback will be trying to get me in control. "Being in control of me in the situation" does *not* mean being in control of you. Being in control of me means that I am not under compulsion—I know I have the choice of giving or not giving feedback.

3. I must be *devoid of judging,* because judging will never be well received.

4. I must be *observant,* so that my feedback follows verifiable observations, not speculations.

5. I must be *clear,* and not contribute to the many potential sources of misunderstanding.

6. I must be *flexible,* able to reframe my feedback into a form the you can understand and accept, rather than always using the same approach.

7. I must *practice,* and learn from my mistakes. That is, I must use feedback about my feedback.

8. I must *become an artist at receiving feedback,* because otherwise I cannot appreciate the difficulties my receiver is experiencing when trying to understand me.

The Art of Receiving Feedback

1. I must *take care of myself,* because if I'm off center, my perceptions and interpretations will be contaminated.

2. I must *feel in control of me in the situation,* because otherwise my energy will be trying to get me in control, rather than understanding your feedback. "Being in con-

trol of me in the situation" does *not* mean being in control of you. Being in control of me means that I am not under compulsion — I know I have the choice of accepting or not accepting feedback.

3. I must be *devoid of judging,* because judging will contaminate my ability to accept or reject feedback on the basis of its information content.

4. I must be *observant*, so that my interpretation follows verifiable observations, not fantasies.

5. I must *seek clarification*, rather than internally amplify the many potential sources of misunderstanding.

6. I must be *flexible,* able to reframe my requests for clarification into a form that you can understand and accept, and able to consider different possibilities for interpretation.

7. I must *practice,* and learn from my mistakes. That is, I must use feedback about my ability to receive feedback.

8. I must become a *feedback artist,* because I cannot be a good receiver of feedback if I have no understanding of the source.

The Art of Congruence

Notice how similar these lists are. That's because to become a feedback artist, I only have to work on me, not on you. That makes the job only half as difficult. In fact, we may have made it seem too difficult. Perhaps all we need is one item that summarizes all the others.

9. Whether giving or receiving feedback, the most important thing is *congruence* — acknowledging, understanding, and accepting what's going on inside of me.

Experiences

1. If you could add one item from your own experience to our "giving" list, what would it be?

2. If you could add one item from your own experience to our "receiving" list, what would it be?

3. If you have important feedback for us, your authors, let us hear from you so that the next book, or next edition, can be a better one.

Appendix A

Designing an Interaction Workshop

The Value of a Workshop Setting This book has attempted to create an environment for learning about giving and receiving feedback in real-life interactions, at work and out of work. Workshops are another excellent environment for both awareness and skill development. A workshop, especially one designed for learning more about yourself and about how you relate to others, provides training opportunities to:

find out how others experience you,

test the effectiveness of your interactions with a wide variety of personalities,

get in touch with your feelings and ways of responding to others.

Workshops are "cultural islands," where your job, career, and personal life are not on the line. Therefore it is possible to examine your strengths and weaknesses in a more "objective" light, to experiment with new behaviors, and to acquire new insights and skills.

There are many workshops already available for these opportunities — for example, workshops on team-building, problem-solving, human interaction, leadership and management skills. All provide settings conducive to learning a great deal more about feedback.

Creating Your Own Workshop But what if you don't have access to one of these workshops? What if you would like to design your own workshop on feedback interactions? You may be a professional educator, or perhaps you just want to construct a feedback workshop for your own work group. Could you really do it?

It's an exciting experience to put together a workshop — and congruent feedback is a crucial professional and personal skill for everyone to attain. It might seem like a difficult job to design and present such a workshop, and we don't mean to imply that it's trivial. But many of our students have succeeded in doing just that. With this book as a guide and source of ideas, you can succeed, too.

The design of your feedback workshop could parallel some of the outline and experiences of our book. This design would include:

the theoretical understanding about giving and receiving feedback

the sequences that help to bring about effective feedback

the self-awareness that is essential to being able to give feedback

opportunity to practice the openness required to accept feedback.

You can, of course, give lectures or little talks in the workshop, but the best talks arise naturally out of the experiences of the workshop. The workshop should include planned skill sessions in which the participants can practice giving and receiving feedback using some of their new learnings and insights.

Also important are those experiences that allow the participants to share the considerable experience with feedback that they bring from their own lives. Feel free to borrow the experiences for these skills sessions and sharing sessions from those given at the end of each chapter. We've tested them, and they work.

In addition, in any experiential workshop, many gems of feedback will appear in the "here and now" settings — whatever is actually going on in the workshop among the participants and that moment. The job of the workshop facilitator is to call attention to those gems and help the participants understand them in terms of the feedback models.

An experiential workshop should be designed to assist participants to continue to learn from their experiences after they leave the workshop setting. In this area, the workshop you design for your co-workers has a great advantage over workshops in far away places, with strangers. The workshop should encourage participants to continue to use their own awareness and skills to experiment and practice using feedback effectively.

If the workshop is given in several small segments, separated by a week or more of "real life," then you can assign "homework" experiences to be brought back to the next meeting and shared with the rest of the group. Some of that "homework" should be to help the participants build the support structures at work and in their personal lives. These support structures would offer them additional resources to continue their own feedback development.

More specific designs to workshops on feedback would be determined by the participant composition, length of workshop, and the particular learning objectives. Let's look at some of the parameters.

Participant Composition One major design choice is between a natural work group and a mixed group of participants. Some advantages of each approach are as follows:

Mixed group

more variety of experiences

less peer pressure, easier to experiment

less old "baggage" to deal with

Natural work group

immediate relevance of experiences

stronger commitment and peer pressure

less warm-up getting to know one another

In general, when training a natural work group, it's useful to have some facilitation from outside the team. Thus, if you are training your own work group, look for an unbiased "outsider" to assist you in keeping old strings untangled.

If you work in a large organization, or belong to a professional society, you may want to consider creating a workshop for special populations. For example, we've done special workshops for accountants, administrators, computer programmers, engineers, nurses, researchers, and sales support staff. Such a workshop has the advantage that you all speak the same language, and have similar experiences and problems to share. If you do create a workshop for such a group, be sure to specialize the activities around their shared language and experience.

Learning Objectives

Feedback learning The obvious objective for a workshop based on this book is simply improving the quantity and quality of feedback. If you have a group that is sufficiently interested in this topic by itself, you can organize along the lines of the book. You won't go far wrong just following the book in sequence, perhaps moving more quickly through sections of less interest to the group.

Team building Often, a natural work team wants to become more effective in working together. A workshop that focuses on feedback, if it contains many practice experiences, will help them to grow and become more resourceful with one another. Quite often, so called "team building" workshops consist solely of feedback theory and experiences.

General Management or Leadership Development When the principal interest of the group is in management issues, you can shape the presentation to that point of view. We've found that managers and those aspiring to become managers get particular benefit out of feedback experiences shaped around the following situations:

performance reviews

interviewing job candidates

making question-and-answer presentations to higher levels of management

handling "difficult" employees

salary and/or responsibility changes as feedback

dealing with the public

Special Issues Feedback can be made the central topic of many so-called "special issues" — such as minority and majority groups, men and women in the workplace, work life versus home life, dual-career couples workshops, or programs for teenagers. Any issue concerning communication between different groups will benefit from improving feedback skills.

Length and Timing

Part of a larger program Because feedback is such an essential ingredient in our growth and development, and the effectiveness of our communications with one another, feedback training is often part of a larger educational/development program. Taking a small piece of an ongoing training program is an excellent way to get yourself started in feedback training. Because it relieves you of much of the responsibility, planning, and administration of an entire workshop, this approach leaves you maximum time to prepare.

What Did You Say? should provide both the substance and experiential activities to be included in any workshop that is concerned with human interaction. Many such programs are overburdened with lectures, and participants will welcome any opportunity you give them to get into interaction with one another — and stop sitting and listening.

Once a week, for one or two hours Holding a sequence of short seminars is another good way to ease into the new task of training people in feedback skills. In the workplace, you can often get an hour or two once a week, even when longer or more frequent periods would be out of the question. (If you can't assemble a group that's willing to give an hour or two a week to the subject, even out of their own time, you don't have a sufficiently motivated audience for a successful workshop. No matter what you do, it's not likely to succeed, so just drop it before you start.)

This format allows you to assign experiences to take place in the interval between meetings. These can include reading assignments, observation of people at work, and experiments with new feedback behaviors.

Once a month, for half or whole day Once you are more experienced at leading seminars, you can work up to giving half or whole day workshops devoted to feedback. You can start with a one-time offering, and if that is successful, offer a monthly experience. You can make assignments for between meetings, but when a month is to go by, people usually put off their assignments and then forget them. When working with a natural work group, however, once-a-month assignments are more likely to succeed — if you give responsibility for the assignments to the group as a whole. A similar effect can be obtained by pairing class members for purposes of homework, because a partner has a motivating effect on most of us.

Two or more days, off site Seminars away from the workplace, and lasting two or more days, are potentially most effective at achieving permanent changes in feedback behavior. Indeed, this is the format your authors prefer. On the other hand, it's probably best not to tackle a workshop this long until you have become an experienced trainer.

When you do reach the point of undertaking a longer seminar, you'll find that *What Did You Say?* is rich enough in theory, examples, and experiences to serve as the backbone of at least a week's worth of intensive work.

We'll Help If We Can Whatever form, content, and audience you decide to tackle, all our best wishes go with you. We'd love to hear from you on how *What Did You Say?* has aided your efforts, and if we can be of any further assistance, drop us a note and we'll try to offer you some feedback on your plans.

Appendix B
Further Resources for
Learning about Feedback

Books

Ashby, W. R., *An Introduction to Cybernetics* (London: Chapman and Hall, 1964).

This book contains the early frameworks of cybernetic or feedback systems.

Bandler, R., & Grinder, J. *Frogs Into Princes: Neuro Linguistic Programming* (Moab, Utah: Real People Press, 1979).

A clear and readable explanation of Neuro Linguistic Programming (NLP), a recently developed theory about how people model their world. NLP was developed from observations of three great therapists in interaction with clients—Virginia Satir, Milton Erickson, and Fritz Perls. NLP can help you understand other peoples' models, thereby improving the quality of both giving and receiving feedback.

Edwards, Betty, *Drawing on the Right Side of the Brain* (Los Angeles: J.P. Tarcher, Inc.,1979).

Edwards explains how she teaches drawing by using the brain model of hemispheric specialization. An excellent book for developing the generally under-used "creative" right hemisphere—for anybody, aspiring artist or not. We have found drawing to be an especially useful technique for breaking through "blocked" feedback situations.

Freedman, Daniel P., and Gerald M. Weinberg, *Handbook of Walkthroughs, Inspections, and Technical Reviews*. (Boston: Little, Brown, 1982).

    Meetings are ritual forms of group interaction which can be designed for different problem solving purposes. This is a handbook on how to design and lead meetings for one often difficult type of feedback—evaluation of work in progress. Such reviews can be a source of growth, or great anxiety and conflict, depending on how they are designed and led.

Freud, Sigmund, *A General Introduction to Psychoanalysis* (New York: Pocket Books, 1975).

    This book is based on a brilliant series of lectures that Freud gave to introduce the then-new concepts of psychoanalysis to medical students. It is particularly interesting in view of the pains that Freud took to overcome the students' resistance to these new ideas, such as the existence of the unconscious.

Keirsey, David and Marilyn Bates, *Please Understand Me: An Essay on Temperament Styles*. (Del Mar, California: Prometheus Nemesis Books, 1978).

    This book gives a detailed and illuminating explanation of the Jungian model of "temperaments." Different temperaments lead to different styles of giving and receiving feedback, and this book is a useful introduction to the subject. It includes a self-administered test and scoring system—a simplified version of the well-known Myers-Briggs Type Indicator. It makes a strong argument for respecting human diversity in personality styles.

Kennedy, Eugene, *On Becoming a Counselor.* (New York: Continuum Publishing Co., 1980).

People who are effective in feedback interactions often find themselves in an unsought role – as counselors to people asking for feedback. Kennedy's book is directed to those who are not professional counselors, but who often perform this function and want to know at least how to give feedback while doing no harm.

Kirschenbaum, Howard, *On Becoming Carl Rogers* (New York: Delacorte Press, 1979).

This is the fullest available biography of Carl Rogers, and how he became Carl Rogers through his passion for listening and learning.

Luft, Joseph, *Of Human Interaction: The Johari Model* (Palo Alto, CA: Mayfield Publishing Co., 1969).

This entire little book is devoted to embellishing the Johari window into "The Johari Model."

Lynch, James J., *The Language of the Heart: The Human Body in Dialogue.* (New York: Basic Books, 1985).

An important and very readable book about the inter-relatedness of language, emotion, and health – how improper feedback can lead to all sorts of sickness. Lynch, a psychologist, makes a convincing case for paying attention to the "social membrane" (human interaction) in understanding and treating hypertension and migraine headaches.

Mayr, Otto, *The Origins of Feedback Control* (Cambridge, MA: The M.I.T. Press, 1970).

This fine little book, nicely translated from the German, explores the many ways the concept of feedback was discovered, or built into inventions, in the centuries before it was articulated by Norbert Weiner.

Mill, Cyril and Larry Porter, ed., *NTL Book of Readings* (Alexandria, VA: NTL Institute, 1989).

This annually-updated collection of 1-3 page essays — on a wide variety of topics relating to interaction in small groups — includes several essays specifically devoted to feedback.

Miller, Alice, *For Your Own Good: Hidden Cruelty in Child-rearing and the Roots of Violence* (New York: Farrar, Straus & Giroux, 1983).

Miller, a Swiss psychiatrist and author, examines how an entire bizarre society — Hitler's Germany — was created through one generation's determined use of critical feedback to children. Among her three individual case studies is the fascinating story of Hitler's own upbringing.

Myers, Isabel Briggs, *Gifts Differing* (Palo Alto, CA: Consulting Psychologists Press, Inc., 577 College Ave., 1980).

Myers, one of the co-designers of the famous Myers-Briggs Type Indicator, explains the Jungian theory behind it. She discusses how to interpret and make practical use of the revealed types, in communication, marriage, learning styles, and occupations. This book could be read profitably in conjunction with Keirsey and Bates, *Please Understand Me.*

Norman, Donald A., *The Psychology of Everyday Things* (New York: Basic Books, 1988).

Don Norman shows how we get feedback from the most common objects in everyday life, like door handles, the controls on television sets and telephones, and how that feedback often surprises us because of the expectations imposed by our mental models. He also shows how such objects could be designed to fit our "natural" models — something which could also be done with our other feedback interactions.

Ranier, Tristine, *The New Diary: How to Use a Journal for Self-Guidance and Expanded Creativity* (New York: St. Martin's Press, 1978).

If you want to learn more about keeping a journal — a way of giving feedback to yourself — here's an excellent book on the subject.

Ritvo, ed., *NTL Managers Handbook* (Alexandria, VA: NTL Institute, 1989).

This is a collection of articles, updated each year, relating to interpersonal skills relevant to managers in organizational settings. The issue of feedback is dealt with as an explicit part of many of the articles.

Rogers, Carl, *Client Centered Therapy: Its Current Practices, Implications, and Theory* (New York: Houghton Mifflin, 1951).

This book gives a good description of the basic counselor responses to a client, with particular emphasis on reflections and clarifications.

...On Personal Power (New York: Dell, 1977).

...On Becoming a Person, (Boston: Houghton Mifflin, 1961) .

This is an excellent general reference to the human potential movement and the psychological processes essential to the healthy development of the individual. A classic in its field, it builds on Rogers' theory of client-centered counseling.

...*A Way of Being* (Boston: Houghton Mifflin, 1980).

Satir, Virginia, *Conjoint Family Therapy. 3rd ed.*(Palo Alto, Ca.: Science and Behavior Books, 1983).

... *Peoplemaking* (Palo Alto, Ca: Science and Behavior Books, 1982).

...*Meditations and Inspirations.,* (Millbrae, Ca.: Celestial Arts, 1985).

...*Your Many Faces.*, (Millbrae, Ca.: Celestial Arts 1978).

...*Making Contact.,*(Millbrae, Ca.: Celestial Arts, 1976).

...*Self-Esteem*. (Millbrae, Ca.: Celestial Arts, 1976).

We have been greatly influenced by the work of Virginia Satir. *Peoplemaking* is a good survey of her ideas about how we learn to interact with others. *Conjoint Family Therapy* is more of a comprehensive textbook for therapists, but like all her books, it is written without academic pretension. All the books are about feedback in one way or another, including *Meditations and Inspirations*, which is a set of wonderful examples of the kind of feedback you can give to yourself. For information concerning her books, workshops, and videotapes, contact: Avanta Network, 139 Forest Avenue, Palo Alto, CA 94301.

Weinberg, Gerald M., *Becoming a Technical Leader* (New York: Dorset House, 1986).

This book is full of ideas on self-development as a leader. It contains additional explanation of the Satir Interaction Model as well as a process for transforming survival rules into "survival guides."

...*An Introduction to General Systems Thinking* (New York: Wiley-Interscience, 1975).

This volume explores the fundamental ideas of systems thinking, with particular emphasis on the difference between perception and interpretation.

...*The Secrets of Consulting* (New York, Dorset House Publishing, Inc., 1985).

Consulting may be defined as the art of influencing people at their request. In short, consulting is paid, professional feedback. *The Secrets of Consulting* takes you behind the scenes of that art, explaining in detail why the world of consulting seems so irrational, and some very practical steps you can take to make it more rational.

...and Daniela Weinberg, *General Principles of System Design* (New York: Dorset House, 1988).

This book shows how many of the deep principles of system design can be derived from the necessity for survival, and how feedback is one of the two great strategies for survival in the natural world.

Weiner, Norbert, *Cybernetics: or Control and Communication in the Animal and the Machine, 2nd Ed.* (Cambridge, MA: The M.I.T. Press, 1961).

A quarter-century ago, this book was judged by a panel of scholars to be one of the books that "most significantly altered the direction of our society" and would "have a substantial impact on public thought and action in the years ahead." They were right.

...*The Human Use of Human Beings: Cybernetics and Society, 2nd, revised ed.* (Garden City, NY: Doubleday Anchor, 1954).

This is the "laymen's version" of *Cybernetics*, in which Weiner draws out some of the wider implications of the earlier, more technical book.

Weisbord, Marvin R., *Productive Workplaces* (San Francisco: Jossey-Bass, Inc., 1987).

Chapters 3 and 4 are the best expositions to date of Lewin's adding action to research.

Williams, Mark, "Lyrics and Music," *Rollercoaster Life* (Washington, DC: Inner Conspiracy Music Company, 1987).

This is an 8-song tape for self-esteem and empowerment that helps us to look inward at ourselves and gets us in touch with the songs within us as a constant resource for feedback to ourselves.

Workshops

NTL Institute, 1240 North Pitt Street, Suite 100, Alexandria, VA 22314-1403

Weinberg and Weinberg, Rural Route Two, Box 33, Lincoln, NE 68520-9417

Index